That's Entertaining

That's Entertaining

RICHARD CAWLEY

Photographs by James Murphy
Original line illustrations by Andrew Whittle

HEADLINE

First published in 1990
by HEADLINE BOOK PUBLISHING PLC

British Library Cataloguing in Publication Data
Cawley, Richard, 1947–
That's entertaining.
1. Food. Recipes
I. Title
641.5

ISBN 0–7472–0169–2

Copy-editor: Lee Faber
Designer: Julia Lilauwala

Printed and bound in Great Britain by
Richard Clay Ltd, Bungay, Suffolk

HEADLINE BOOK PUBLISHING PLC
Headline House
79 Great Titchfield Street
London W1P 7FN

FOR JANE

Acknowledgements

I would like to particularly thank my two excellent and invaluable assistants, Martha Holmberg, who helped plan the menus, test the recipes and type the original manuscript, and Ian Hands, who helped me with the cooking and styling for all the photographs.

'There are parties and parties! For Christmas and Easter and Halloe'en; for birthdays and May-days; for strawberry-time and hay-time, and last but not least for fun! You give these when you feel so good that you simply can't keep it all to yourself!
From 'When You Give a Party' by
M. V. Jack in The Children's Golden
Treasure Book *(Odhams, 1948)*

Contents

A Preview

 MY EARLIEST memory of being entertained is not of being taken to some other child's birthday party – in fact, I don't think I really liked children's parties – but of occasional visits to my mother's dressmaker. I was probably only four, and although I can't picture the dressmaker herself, I can vividly remember how I loved her tiny house and the gorgeous warm feeling of being spoiled. The parlour was small and cosy and crowded with old-fashioned ornaments. It seemed that everything about that room was either knitted or crocheted or embroidered. Except, that is, the black-leaded iron range with its glowing coals, murmuring kettle and sleeping cat.

Whilst my mother and the dressmaker closeted themselves away in another fascinating room, full of bright cotton reels, paper patterns and scraps of gay cotton prints, I was left on a little stool by the fire to enjoy my milk and biscuits, with the cat and a loudly ticking clock for company. I was quite happy to just sit and be 'grown up' in someone else's house and jiggle my small shoes into the thick rag rug.

Things were rather different when my mother entertained at home. There I wasn't spoiled, but I was allowed to join the guests in the front room if I was quiet and well behaved. It would be morning coffee or afternoon tea, and although it might only be Auntie Dorothy and Auntie Peg, everything had to be 'just right'.

In the mornings, guests were served a beverage of powdered coffee and hot milk in a tall, elaborate silver coffee pot. My mother didn't actually like it at all, but it was apparently the thing to serve in the early fifties. Afternoon tea was better, with scones and cakes and Melting Moments – all home-made, of course. I don't think the teapot was silver, but there were lace paper doilies on the plates and my mother would wear one of her bright cotton dresses made from a paper pattern, fitted in that little back room and patterned with poodles, or Paris scenes or splashy abstracts (my father didn't like flowers). I would lie quiet as a mouse behind the settee, in case I should be told to go and play. I loved it all; the best china and the front room behaviour. It seemed so sophisticated, the incomprehensible gossip and talk of Continental holidays.

1

The only big parties I remember were at Christmas. These would be mostly family affairs, but there would usually be one or two extra guests around the festive table. Christmas lunch was the most important meal of the year and my mother would begin the preparations months in advance, bringing back big bunches of marjoram from the market in late summer to dry, ready for the turkey's delicious stuffing. The fruit for the puddings and mincemeat would also be washed and laid out on clean tea towels to be dried. It seemed very odd to me to be making Christmas puddings in midsummer, but at least it registered that it is never too early to begin planning and organising a party if it is to be a success.

First thing on the morning of the great day itself, the wide oak table in the dining room would be laid. The three extra leaves would be added and then the table would be spread, first with a thick fringed cloth of blood red chenille and then with starched white damask and polished silver. Thus organised, my mother's time was spent doing the last minute jobs of vegetables and gravy and whisky sauce for the pudding. The meal was a masterpiece of planning and organisation, and the food was, of course, superb. Every year at the end of the meal, my father would compliment my mother with 'Well, we might make a cook of you yet', and my grandfather would repeat his much-loved trick of pretending to choke on a sixpence from the pudding before handing out his customary largesse to us kids.

Nobody, I think, relished my mother's Christmas meal more than she did herself, and from her I have learned the very satisfying habit of really enjoying my own cooking. Now, if complimented on some successful dish, I am likely to reply as she might, with 'Yes, it did turn out rather well'. I am always irritated by people who apologise for their cooking – they shouldn't invite guests if they are going to cook something they aren't happy with.

My big sister's Twenty-First celebration, when I was eleven, was altogether a different matter and much less traditional. Christine was studying domestic science in London, and her party had to be a much more modern and sophisticated affair – a buffet with 'Continental' salads and the like. She and her friends wore dresses that stuck right out over lurid-coloured net petticoats, and they danced with their boyfriends to Pat Boone and Frank Sinatra records. I was allowed to stay up and was delirious with joy. I loved the glamour of it all – the fancy food, the sticking-out petticoats and the smoochy music. So, apparently, did my sister's beau, and they got engaged, to be married.

The wedding was my first peek into a new world of entertaining on a grand scale. Never before was such glamour and sophistication dreamed of, never before had there been such a gala celebration – or so I imagined then, and at last I understood why those interminable weeks of talking and planning and list-making had been so necessary. The sun shone and the church was packed. My sister was radiant in ivory brocade and tulle; my mother, both regal and tottering in fur stole and the very latest in white winkle-picker shoes. Even my then-despised elder brother was transformed into a film star in top hat and tails.

The two most elegant guests at the wedding, however, were without any doubt in our minds myself and my best friend. I wore my first suit, the bottom half of which consisted of my first long trousers. My friend gained rather less satisfaction from her sartorial first as it was concealed beneath girlish gingham and wasn't as yet strictly necessary, seeming to cause her more discomfort than pleasure, as did her first pair of real stockings. Not too much to spoil our fun, however, nor to prevent us from squeezing every last bit of enjoyment out of the 'reception' at the hotel at the smarter end of the town.

The wedding lunch remained printed in my mind for a long time afterwards. The serried ranks of shining cutlery, the endless succession of courses, the waitresses and the formality, the top table, the rows of people in elegant clothes, the speeches and, of course, the cake. Here I learned for the first time the effect of original touches when entertaining. On the very top of this spectacular many-tiered confection perched a small silver vase of flowers. Nothing as ordinary as rosebuds or carnations for my sister, but something, I learned, called stephanotis which smelt sublime. I wasn't the only one impressed by the cake's decoration, and the stephanotis received compliments throughout the day.

Very early on I discovered what a joy it is to sample something different, and how pleasant it feels if someone makes an effort to give you a treat. My earliest guide and mentor in this respect was my music teacher. After I passed a piano exam she invited me to tea, as a little celebration. I was fascinated, shocked and thrilled to be offered 'Indian or China?'. I didn't know quite what this meant, but thought China sounded more exotic. It had never occurred to me that there was more than one kind of tea. I was given my first cup of Earl Grey. It

tasted so different from what we drank at home, but I thought I rather liked it and determined there and then that I was going to try anything new that I might be offered in the future, but above all, that when I was grown-up I would always offer 'Indian or China?'.

Fanny Cradock was the TV cook of the day. I knew that appearances were important, as my mother would remove her pinny and pat her hair as she passed the mirror on the way to answer the front door or even the telephone, but Fanny's hair never needed patting and she certainly never wore a pinny. I would watch enthralled whilst she flambéed and garnished and demonstrated, without getting a crumb of pastry in her large glittering rings or a spot of fat on her draped white chiffon or beaded satin. I gathered that when entertaining in style, nothing can be too fancy! I now know that this need not always be the case, and that indeed, simplicity is often preferable, but my close friends and family will attest that I do not always practise what I preach!

At the age of eighteen I was sent off to Paris to study fashion design. After having lived in a very provincial Yorkshire market town, it certainly would have been hard to keep me 'down on the farm' after I'd seen 'Paree'. I simply couldn't believe that Paris was as enormous, beautiful and glamorous as it turned out to be, and I began quickly to soak up a lot more than fashion design. I lived with a French family in their Art Nouveau villa on the outskirts of the city. Circumstances had become reduced at some recent time, forcing them to leave their château in the countryside for this smaller suburban residence. Monsieur was a bank manager and Madame was a 'lady' and although they were very kind to me, and I was terribly impressed by the Aubusson rugs, and the oil paintings of eighteenth-century ancestors, their

life style was a little too precise even for my newly 'sophisticated' tastes.

Dinner each evening was lengthy and very formal. Didine, the maid, waited on and the conversation was 'polite'. It fascinated me that everything was served separately, whereas at home we had eaten our meat and vegetables all off one plate. I grew to like tasting each component of the meal separately, and the food was always delicious, but I soon grew impatient at having to spend so long at the dinner table, particularly as I was obliged always to wear a jacket and tie.

When at last we did retire to the pretty drawing-room for coffee and liqueurs, I always felt that the ancestors were scowling down at me from their gilt carved frames in case I should spill a drop of coffee on the priceless needlework chairs.

My parents were adamant that at nineteen, I was far too young to have a flat of my own when I moved next to London to continue my studies. Consequently, my digs were awful. I lodged with a Dickensian family who rowed constantly. Their incessant shouting rose through the floor of my dingy room, along with the smells of overcooked food. Not only were there no maids, no linen sheets and no Aubusson rugs, but every day I was brought cold spaghetti hoops on soggy toast for breakfast by a tear-stained daughter of the house.

This last fact was my saving grace, as my mother, horrified by such culinary grossness, persuaded my father that I could move into a flat of my own. It was there in that tiny apartment in the East End of London that I began to learn about entertaining, albeit the hard way.

To help with expenses during my student days, I occasionally babysat for some family friends. The money, of course, was very useful, but even though I was thrilled to have my own flat, I just loved the beautiful Hampstead house where my employers lived.

It was these kind people who invited me to my first grown-up dinner party and I was terribly impressed. The conversation was of plays and books and childbirth and seemed so sophisticated. The table looked lovely and we ate a superb leg of lamb, with green beans – no potatoes! This was followed by a simple salad, then fruit and cheese. The organisation, the food, the whole evening was quite perfect – the hostess hardly left the table – but it was some time before I was to learn from her good example.

I returned my sophisticated friends' invitation at the earliest opportunity and was determined to impress. *Harengs en Papilotte* sounded just the thing, I thought, and after briefly reading the recipe, I dashed off to the fishmonger to buy three herrings. In my haste I had not noticed the bit in the recipe which said 'cleaned'.

It took me quite some time to disembowel the unfortunate creatures, as I had to leave my tiny kitchen every few seconds to sit down on the bed to recover from the waves of nausea. Eventually, feeling miserable and exhausted, I managed to stuff the poor fish with the onions and mushrooms and whatever, wrap them in foil and throw them in the oven just as the doorbell rang. It was the first time I had ever used the oven, and it hadn't occurred to me to see if there was anything inside it. Whatever the previous tenant had left in there, it had been there for a while, and soon my little bedsit was filled with evil-smelling smoke. My guests were as understanding about this as they were about the food, which tempered my mortification. The important lesson in the art of entertaining learned from this fiasco was that it is just as important to be a good guest as a good host.

A good many years have passed since my first disastrous attempt at entertaining, and I am pleased to report that I've been making progress ever since. Despite the occasional flop here and there I've learnt an enormous amount and had a lot of fun in the process. I've also been very fortunate in that I have managed to travel a good deal, visiting many other parts of the world and learning about different ways of cooking and entertaining.

I have eaten extraordinary Oriental delicacies at a lavish Chinese banquet given by the captain of a Yangtse cruise ship, feasted on Australian mud crabs at an elegant Sydney lunch party and even been wined and dined on one unforgettable occasion at Château Mouton Rothschild in Bordeaux, but, funnily enough, it is the simpler occasions which stick out in my mind, like the time when, as a backpacking student, I travelled to the east of Turkey by bus.

We were in the remote and primitive town of Diyabakir, close to the borders of Syria and Russia. It was the first time I had ever felt nervous in Turkey – earlier in the day, children had thrown stones at us in the street. In the hot, dusty main square, a young blind man approached us. He was neat and clean, but wore the poorest of patched clothes. Attracted by our English voices, he asked if he could walk with us to practise his English. A friend, he told us proudly, was a barber who had a radio and allowed him to listen every morning to an English station.

He led us back to the old part of the city and asked if he could treat us to a cup of tea. We were embarrassed because we knew that the strict Turkish customs of hospitality would not allow us to pay and he would have been very hurt if we had refused his offer.

We nervously followed him down dark alleyways and through dusty courtyards, then through a maze of narrow passageways into the depths of the covered bazaar. The tea shop was no more than a dark, grubby little room full of men. Some were blind, some were crippled and all were poor. These circumstances were in no way embarrassing to them, however, they were simply pleased to have the opportunity to offer some hospitality to guests.

Some old stools were pulled up for us and dusted down. Little chipped cups of tea were pressed into our hands. An old man rolled a few of his precious strands of tobacco into a little square of paper and stuck it down very thoroughly with a studied lick. The tea was only warm and sickly sweet and I found it very difficult to smoke the choking little cigarette, but I will never forget being entertained by those kind people who had so little to give, who taught me what immense pleasure even the simplest gesture of hospitality can give to both the giver and the receiver.

Although coloured or patterned plates can look very attractive, plain white tableware is much more versatile (if you only have one set) and, with the addition of a few simple props, your whole table setting can quickly change to suit the menu or the occasion. In these photographs the absolutely plain white plates are a classic Wedgwood design and those with the narrow gold banding were bought surprisingly cheaply from a high street chain store.

1. Avocado Salad with Walnuts and Caper–Lemon Dressing (*see page* 94).

2. Lychees in Green Ginger Wine (*see page* 111).

3. Chicken in Herb and Lemon Sauce in Pastry Baskets (*see page* 57).

4. Jellied Caviare and Soured Cream Consomme (*see page* 64).

5. Water Chestnuts in Crispy Bacon . . . Chicken Satay . . . Coriander Lamb in Filo Packets (*see pages* 32–33).

6. Filo Pastry Purses with Salmon and Spring Onions (*see page* 84).

Entertaining Prospects

 ENTERTAINING does not always need careful planning. Even impromptu parties can become really memorable occasions.

An unexpectedly fine weekend might provoke an urge to put away the gardening tools and suggest a last-minute barbecue with all the guests joining in the cooking – what could be more fun? Some friends might drop in on their way back from their holidays with a present of some local charcuterie or sun-drenched tomatoes. How pleasant it can be to throw a cloth on the table, light some candles, rustle up a simple meal and sit down to share the last of your visitors' holiday happiness.

When your party-giving is premeditated, rather than spur of the moment, you owe your guests some degree of organisation. If you invite close friends for a casual meal, warning that dinner will be served on trays in front of the TV, that's perfectly fine. However, I personally dislike more than anything being invited to what I have been led to believe will be a proper meal, only to find Clare in gardening clothes, rummaging in the freezer for a vegetable and be told that 'Tim won't be back for ages as he had to take the kids swimming'.

The reverse situation is equally embarrassing. It is most disconcerting to arrive, bottle of plonk in hand, wearing a sweater and jeans and expecting a plate of pasta by the fire, to have the door opened by an elegantly dressed, coiffed and perfumed hostess and be introduced to a roomful of strangers dressed in suits, frocks and jewellery.

It is essential, therefore, when inviting people for an occasion of any kind, to make it perfectly clear what kind of party it is – how formal, how much or little food there will be, how many other people will be there and who they are. If you normally eat with the children at six and want to invite someone round for the evening at eight for a few drinks, do make it understood that you have already eaten, or your unfortunate guests are in for an embarrassing evening of tummy rumbles and will probably end up dead drunk. Great discomfort can be caused by forgetting to tell a guest that the party you are inviting them to is, in fact, a surprise fortieth birthday celebration for your partner or spouse, or that you had decided this year it might be fun if everyone came to your Christmas party dressed in red.

As even your best friend can't always read your mind, the simplest way to convey all this important information is via a written invitation. People are accustomed to receiving written invitations to formal occasions such as weddings, but should you – and why shouldn't you? – send out printed invitations to a moderate-sized lunch or dinner party (well-photocopied is very simple and affordable), your friends might be a bit surprised, but thrilled and flattered that you are putting on such a posh show for them. As a result, they'll arrive looking the part and behave accordingly. Even with written invitations, a quick telephone call is sometimes a good idea to make sure the guests have in fact received the invitations and to communicate 'extra' information such as 'we thought it might be fun to all get dressed up and have a proper party', or 'it's been such a long dreary winter', 'Trevor just sold his first article to the local newspaper', 'my geranium cuttings have finally taken!'.

THE CAST

When it comes to deciding just who you are actually going to invite to your event, be brave and don't just ask the same friends every time. Why not invite your fishmonger if he always makes you laugh, or the friendly woman who you chat to at your aerobics class, or that interesting couple with a small landscape gardening business that you met at Jack and Alice's one Sunday lunchtime? Remember that giving a good party is like putting on a theatrical production. As host, you are not only the producer, director, designer and stage manager, but also the casting director, so choose your players very carefully. It isn't sufficient to clean the house, set the table attractively and provide good food. Really memorable occasions are produced by the right chemistry between the guests. Think of the parties you remember most and you will invariably remember who was there rather than what you ate or drank.

A dinner party of three or four couples of approximately the same age, with similar life styles and interests will most probably be pleasant, but an eclectic mix of guests could provoke more stimulating conversation and provide just the electricity to make a really memorable evening. Don't feel that the very young will necessarily find the elderly boring and stuffy, or that a more mature person will find a student too naive to make good company. Remember, also, that not everyone is half of a couple. It is totally unnecessary to have an even number of each sex seated alternatively around your table.

Party-giving is a wonderful way of both keeping in touch with old chums, making new ones and also; a good circle of interesting friends is more valuable that anything money can buy and well worth nurturing.

WHYS AND WHEREFORES

It is a good idea at this early planning stage to decide in your own mind exactly why you are giving a party so that you can decide on the best kind of affair. Should it be large or small, formal or informal, should you have it at home or hire a hall, dare you risk planning an outdoor event? There are so many different kinds of parties and so many different reasons for giving them. Birthdays, anniversaries and other celebrations naturally call for a party, and you might want to plan around a theme. This is a great idea for children's parties, but other events can also be made that bit more special by adding to the romance of the occasion with a special theme. It might be fun, when planning a drinks party for the office or for business acquaintances, to make the occasion more lighthearted and really go with a swing by suggesting a 1920s cocktail party with drinks to match. Or why not plan a college reunion and suggest that everyone comes dressed in 'period'? Fashions of the fifties or sixties, or even the seventies can be easily rustled up, and many people – even the normally shy ones – adore dressing up. Most people love to be invited to a fancy-dress ball, which could be a wonderful fund-raising ploy. It is not too difficult to achieve with an enthusiastic committee and makes a refreshing change from bazaars, sponsored swims and coffee mornings. More on themes later.

Holidays provide good excuses for party-giving, Christmas and New Year being the obvious ones, but what about giving a Guy Fawkes party, a Valentine's Day dinner, a harvest festival supper or just a lovely al fresco feast to celebrate midsummer? Lunch and dinner are the usual times for party-giving, but Sunday breakfast with all the wonderful traditional British food that goes with it – and of course all the newspapers – can be

great fun and a perfect way for people with children to get together. If breakfast sounds a bit too early in the day, invite your guests a little later for an American brunch; then you can serve Bloody Marys as well as coffee and tea. Afternoon tea is a delightful meal which deserves reviving as a party idea.

It might be that your only excuse for throwing a party is that you have learned to cook some delicious new thing and want to show off. If so, don't invite relative strangers to witness your little performance or you may fall flat on your face, and be rewarded with such comments as 'How clever of you to attempt this *without* the truffles . . .' or maybe 'Isn't it nice to get back to good plain food?'. Only perform your latest acts for very close friends or family you can be sure will appreciate the effort you have made for them, share in your triumphant moment, and give you the rewarding little pat on the back you have worked so hard for.

THE MASTER PLAN

Now, having decided what kind of party you are going to give, who you are going to invite and why you are doing it, the next step towards success is to assess your limitations and design a master plan. Your main restrictions will be those of money, skill, time and space, plus any likes or dislikes of your guests. This may not just apply to food! If Auntie Alice is allergic to animals, don't ask her for lunch on the day your Siamese has just had a litter of six, or force your painfully shy adolescent nephew to talk to a ravishing extrovert actress at your New Year buffet party.

Money limitations are often hard to admit and boring to think about, but straightforward to sort out if you just follow this simple little plan. First, work out exactly how much you can honestly afford (or are prepared) to spend on the occasion, then do a few calculations. Decide on what drinks you want to serve – this is always the most expensive item – and subtract the cost from the total. Then take away any other expenditures – the cost of flowers or candles, or a special piece of kitchen equipment, or something new to wear. The total you are left with is the amount you can spend on the food. It will no doubt seem surprisingly little, but if you ignore such extravagances as out-of-season strawberries and asparagus and fillet of beef, it is extraordinary how little you will need to spend per head to put on a really good spread. Often I have managed to feed six at home for what it would cost for one in an average-priced restaurant.

If money is no object, it is the easiest thing in the world to produce a fabulous meal, and can take next to no time. Expensive cuts of meat, and fish like salmon, turbot or giant prawns need very little doing to them. I should personally, if I could afford it, feel very happy to serve my dinner guests a huge platter of hot, fresh English asparagus, dripping with the best butter, followed perhaps by a lobster each, then Roquefort cheese with some really special red wine, finishing off with chilled dishes of wild strawberries. It would, of course, cost a great deal of money and it would take up very little of my time, effort, skill or imagination. It is with these four elements, however, that you must be prepared to be lavish if, like mine, your purse is not bottomless. Your beautiful, slow-cooked casserole, aromatic with home-grown herbs, your spectacular home-made puff pastry, or a delicious salad made with a really imaginative combination of ingredients will please your guests just as much as any meal laden with luxury ingredients.

Any special skills you have should be utilised to the fullest. If you happen to be good at boning chicken, get boning, or if you are a good bread maker, fill the house with the inimitable smell of baking to greet your guests and set their taste buds working. A friend's mother, who is also a potter, found she could further utilise her skills by making perfect, tiny hand-raised pork pies, which are in constant demand by friends and family. If your back garden is bursting with flowers, make a gorgeous centrepiece for the table. Such skills are not only money-saving, but extremely rewarding in themselves and always successful, as they show your guests that you've added that extra personal touch.

However, it is very important to be practical and honest with yourself, and not to bite off more than you can chew. If

you are a relative newcomer to kitchen matters, don't be tempted – no matter how eager to please you might be – to cook something too difficult. Daring to be simple is one of the hardest lessons to learn. The most obvious, yet most common mistake made by even the more experienced of us, is to cook something you haven't tried before. Your oven temperature may not be the same, your flour the same quality, or your gelatine have the same setting power as those of the person who wrote the recipe; even a printing error might lead to a disaster. I have on occasion tried a new recipe which sounded great, only to find it deadly dull, or even revolting! Recipes that contain any element of risk or doubt should be put firmly from your mind, no matter how intriguing they might sound. If you simply must try them, conduct such experiments only on your family or closest of friends who won't mind too much if things go miserably wrong.

Most of us find spare time as difficult to come by as spare cash, but it is important to realise when embarking on any entertaining plans, be they small or large, that it takes a certain amount of time in advance to entertain but, more importantly, that the work doesn't finish when the doorbell rings. With very few exceptions, the party giver must be on duty until the very end if the proceedings are going to be a complete success. Brillat-Savarin, a witty and wise gourmet and philosopher of the nineteenth century, put this fact so succinctly when he wrote 'To entertain a guest is to make yourself responsible for his happiness as long as he is beneath your roof'.

Even when planning a party on a very modest scale, if you allow yourself *more* than enough time, your efforts should reward you with pleasure rather than become an exhausting chore, and you will get as much out of the occasion as your lucky guests. If you feel that this will

not be the case, and you cannot devote adequate time, don't entertain, because if it appears obvious that no pleasure has been gained from giving, certainly none will be gained by the receiver.

The biggest time-waster is lack of organisation. Even those with the most ordered minds and retentive memories will benefit immeasurably from the careful writing of lists – lists of jobs, shopping lists and lists of cooking schedules. We all forget something at some stage and it is difficult to make an omelette without eggs. On one occasion when I hadn't bothered to write a guest list, I just kept counting the names on my fingers and repeatedly ending up with the number eight, thus setting the table and preparing the food for that number. However, when we came to sit down to eat, we were two places and two helpings short – I had forgotten to include the two party-givers in my mental jottings! Now I make lists and more lists, and when those are all ticked off, still more lists. Those last-minute little jobs might seem straightforward and simple as you lie in the bath with a much-deserved gin and tonic at 7.30, but by 8.30 with the guests all talking to you at once, things don't always seem quite so clear. How reassuring then to be comforted by the sight of large, clearly-written lists over the cooker telling you that at 8.45 you

Jean-Anthelme Brillat-Savarin was a gourmet philosopher who was born in the French town of Belley in 1755 and became its mayor in 1793. He fled from the Revolution first to Switzerland and then America, earning his living giving French lessons and playing in a theatre orchestra. He returned to his native land in 1796, and his famous book, *La Physiologie du goût*, was published in 1825.

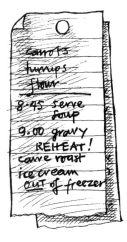

must serve the soup, turn up the oven and put in the Yorkshires, and at 9.00 you must reheat the gravy, carve the roast and transfer the ice cream from the freezer to the fridge. How very satisfying it is also at the end of the meal, when you remove the debris to the kitchen to find the tray that you have so efficiently set, ready for tea and coffee, and not have to fumble around looking for the camomile tea bags or those elusive filter papers.

CROWD SCENES

You don't need a lot of space to give a party. For years I managed to entertain in very cramped circumstances, and one of my most successful dinner parties was whilst living in a tent by a river in the south of France, with only two camping gas rings and a tiny table. When space is limited, only a little imagination is needed, as well as careful and tidy organisation. Remember, if your guests are being entertained in the dining room, they can't see whatever havoc might be in the kitchen or hear you cursing and swearing as the toast for the pâté burns for the seventh time. Eating in the kitchen can be a very cosy and friendly way of entertaining, but remember that the cook cannot then go 'backstage' and

the whole performance is seen. Remember also that no matter how informal the occasion, nobody wants to witness a violent drama when they are prepared for light entertainment, nor do they want to dine staring at a mountain of dirty pans, or go home with their best clothes smelling of deep-fried mushrooms, no matter how good they tasted. So if your guests are going to be seated on the stage all evening with you, plan the performance and the menu accordingly.

Most of us should be able to manage, by careful budgeting and planning, to produce a memorable dinner party for six or eight people, as they don't take up too much space, don't cost too much to feed and are an ideal number for good round-the-table conversation. However, a few years ago, I found a splendid Victorian oak table in a second-hand shop at a very good price. By means of a large metal cranking handle which fits into one end and three separate leaves, it can change from a pleasant average-sized dining table to an expansive setting for twelve. Some serious junk shop hunting turned up twelve rather battered-looking, but plain stacking chairs, which were transformed with a coat of cream egg-shell paint. When I do get round to making the striped cotton tie-on seat cushions, they will look quite handsome, but meanwhile they are more than adequate. I now love to occasionally give a dinner party for twelve. Somehow the table set with all the rows of glasses and plates twinkling in the candlelight looks quite magical, and my friends love the sense of occasion. The fashion for so long has been to entertain informally that everyone now relishes a bit of a change and loves the opportunity to get dressed up. Chairs don't have to match, of course, and two trestle tables put together and covered with pretty sheets or a length of cheap dress fabric will do the job just as well.

The best thing about giving these large dinners is that they seem to take up hardly more time and energy than a much smaller meal, and certainly food for one dinner for twelve costs considerably less, for some reason, than two dinners for six. The washing up afterwards is rather boring, and I somehow feel that it is a comedown, if a party has been a real success, to have guests helping around the sink, but only you can make those kinds of decisions . . .

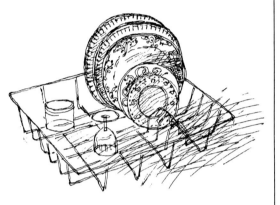

Even really sizeable parties can be quite manageable so long as they aren't for very formal occasions. My most successful large party was for eighty art students in my house. I had very little time or money to spend, but wanted it to be really special. I kept the food very simple, but there needed to be lots of it, and I managed to produce adequate mountains of two hot dishes – one based on 'bargain' chicken wings, bought in bulk, and the other a tasty and very inexpensive casserole based on vegetables for the non-meat eaters. With lots of baked potatoes, good bread and salad, eighty young and very healthy appetites were satisfied for an amazingly small amount of money.

If you have something very special to celebrate, and don't find it necessary to entertain on a strict budget, you can employ professionals to do the work for you, but even this will need a lot of your own time spent getting the organisation perfect, so that none of your hard-earned money is wasted. Look in the Yellow Pages or local magazines and newspapers for caterers and hire firms. Word of mouth or recommendation is the safest way of finding someone good. If you find the food and organisation at someone else's cocktail party or wedding to your liking, find out who they used.

One of the best such parties I have been to was a friend's fortieth birthday. The couple live in the country and had hired a large barn attached to a pub. The attractive old building had a roaring, open log fire at one end and was decorated with giant arrangements of greenery from some recent tree prunings. The atmosphere was one of constant hilarity from the word go, as the invitation had suggested the mode of dress as 'bizarre'. The food was provided by the pub, and was an enormous success, because apart from the usual salads and side dishes, a large barbecue was set up outside, sensibly under a canvas cover in case of rain. After much laughter and dancing, our appetites were more than whetted for delicious grilled chops and sausages, and best of all, barbecued whole trout, an original and very popular alternative to meat.

Such a party could be very successfully achieved in a much less expensive DIY way if you can find a village, church or school hall for hire which has a bit of open ground. A temporary barbecue can easily be made with some old bricks and metal grills, but this kind of cooking and entertaining cannot be achieved single-handedly, and you will need to organise several willing helpers to share the work. There are lots of good books specialising in barbecues and outdoor cookery, so it's best to swot up on the matter first, and practise on a small scale to get your cooking temperatures just right. No one likes chicken legs that are burnt black on

the outside and cold and red raw in the middle.

If your budget won't stretch to hiring staff to help and serve at your party, don't put the idea completely out of your mind. Students and young relatives are often only too pleased to earn a little extra pocket money, and will cost you considerably less than professionals. Perhaps your babysister might enjoy being a cocktail waitress for the same rate per hour.

Then, of course, there is free labour. Husbands, wives and other partners will share the work (unless you have chosen badly, that is!), but don't be too proud to ask other friends to help. It can also be fun to plan a party with someone else, and you should end up with half the work and double the pleasure. Quite small children can perform simple tasks very well under supervision, and most of them love being given adult responsibilities. Their small fingers are often very nimble at performing fiddly culinary feats, and could make short work of some repetitive task, leaving your hands free for other jobs. Children also make very good waiters and waitresses. It is an excellent way of keeping them amused and out of trouble at mainly adult func-

tions, particularly at drinks parties where it is important that the drinks and nibbles be constantly circulated.

For really large formal occasions like weddings, catering, organising and serving is best done by professionals. But if your guest list is a managebale number, you might prefer the intimacy of giving the party yourself in a hired hall, or in your home perhaps with the help of a marquee. Even a sit-down wedding meal is quite feasible with a little help and a lot of meticulous organisation. You will be certain to produce a much more personal and original celebration than a similar function put on by professionals.

A final word, from personal experience, on giving large parties. Although help-yourself buffets might seem the easiest way to cope with large numbers, if there is any way that you can manage to get all your guests sitting down at a table with a knife and fork in front of them and have them served with their food instead of helping themselves, not only will the event feel more special, but you will have more control over the proceedings, and be able to see at a glance that everyone has food and someone to talk to.

The celebration for my father's eightieth birthday was a perfect example. A party in an hotel was ruled out by the family as being too impersonal and yet some degree of formality was called for on such an important occasion. With us four children sharing the catering and organisation, and working to a plan of almost military precision, we managed to produce a rather impressive sit-down lunch for eighty people.

The village hall was raided for ten round tables and sufficient chairs, plates and cutlery; the sitting-room of the rambling old mill where my older brother lives was emptied of all its usual furniture, then, with the help of checked cloths and pretty arrangements of garden flowers for each table, we managed to create a 'French bistro' which spilled out into the wide hallway.

Luckily the sun put on a pretty good show and the elegantly dressed guests were able to enjoy their pre-lunch drinks in the garden whilst the unpaid 'staff' of small grandchildren put the finishing touches to the tables and set a plate of avocado and seafood terrine by each carefully placed name card. The terrine, the rest of the food and the festivities in general were voted by all to have been a huge success, and although economy had not been our prime concern, the party cost a fraction of the price that it would had we hired professionals, but best of all, because of sensible delegation, no one had that much work to do.

Most of all, the Octogenarian thought it was the best surprise party ever and was glad that he had splashed out on a particularly dapper new double-breasted suit for the occasion!

PREPARATIONS

When entertaining, food is only part of what the host should offer his guests. 'To break bread' with visitors at your table is the most ancient way of offering hospitality and demonstrating friendship. If you offer food to a guest, it should be the very best that you can provide in the circumstances, a theory that Brillat-Savarin expressed so well when he wrote: 'The man who invites his friends to his table and fails to give his personal attention to the meal they are going to eat is unworthy to have friends.' But first, everything must be prepared.

Equipment

Unless you are going to buy all your food for a party ready-prepared, the kitchen is the most important room in an 'entertainer's' life. Obviously, the more space and the better the equipment you have,

the easier your cooking tasks will be. Nonetheless, superb meals can come out of the tiniest cooking areas, with the most basic equipment. However, if you are going to entertain regularly, it is important to provide yourself with the best equipment you can afford. There are so many new gadgets on the market, it is very difficult to know what is going to be a sensible, enduring buy, and what might be relegated to a jumble sale before too long; like the intriguing device I once bought at the Ideal Home Exhibition which could transform potatoes, carrots, cucumbers and no end of other edibles into long spirals I could never quite find a use for.

You must use your judgement and buy your kitchen wizards to suit your own taste and life style. If you are passionate about home-made pasta, a hand-cranked pasta machine might soon become your favourite friend in the kitchen, and if your family adore yogurt, a yogurt maker might save you a lot of money. The biggest fridge you can afford and have space for is advisable. A freezer is useful, but not essential to many people; however, it is certainly a boon for those who want to entertain and don't have much time, as you can cook dishes ahead, and also stock it with things like cooked pastry cases, stocks, soups, pâtés (which can

quickly form part of a speedy, effortless meal) and ice cream, which is always a satisfactory and popular instant pudding.

If you are at home all day with plenty of time on your hands, a microwave will probably not be very useful, but microwaves and other electrical equipment can make entertainment easy for busy hosts. I love my slow cooker, which can be filled in the morning and provide a delicious hot meal all ready in the evening when I come home after a busy day. It's also very useful for making stocks. The carcass of a chicken eaten one evening will provide the stock to make a delicious soup or risotto the next. If you are at the very beginning of your carrer as an 'entertainer' you may have to manage with the most basic equipment, but do not be deterred, as jumble sales and junk shops are an excellent source of cheap second-hand kitchen goods, which once thoroughly cleaned, will probably soon become firm friends and serve you for years.

Shopping

To produce good food, shopping for the best, freshest and cheapest ingredients is as important as combining and cooking them. Naturally, the more food that you can buy close to the time you want to use it, the better. You must fight the temptation to overbuy, so if you see some stunningly fresh artichokes at a bargain price on Saturday, but know you won't need them until Monday, resist the urge to stock up; perhaps on Monday you will find some particularly fresh asparagus. With the odd exceptions, like well-aged beef and game, which are better for being hung, you can be sure that the fresher food is, the more delicious it will taste. Those lucky enough to have gardens in which to grow vegetables will know just how much better they taste if picked just minutes before cooking. Even the tiniest plot of earth could provide

you with your own beans or raspberries, and a 'grow bag' on a patio, roof or balcony will yield a surprising amount of tomatoes or herbs. In addition to the better flavour, you will have the added enjoyment of eating your own produce. Those with no access to outdoor space will gain great pleasure from a few pots of fragrant basil or glossy green peppers on sunny window ledges.

Even the freshest produce at your greengrocer's or local market will be at least one day old (and probably a lot more). Food in supermarkets is often fresher because they usually have their own transportation and a quicker turnover, but if, like me, you want to support your local small shopkeepers, pick out your favourites and cultivate them. A faithful customer will always get better service and a more honest answer when asking how fresh something is, which you must never be afraid to do. It is equally important, if you have been particularly pleased with the quality of some meat or the freshness of some vegetables, to thank and compliment your butcher and greengrocer when you next see them. This way you will build up an honest and fruitful relationship with the people who supply your ingredients.

I hardly need point out the wisdom of choosing all your food as free of additives and as unprocessed as possible. This doesn't just apply to packaged foods, as even innocent-looking vegetables have often been tampered with – not only are chemicals sometimes sprayed onto fruits or vegetables; they are also present in the earth in which they are grown. I think the extra money spent on free-range eggs is worth it, both for the taste and because the poor hens get a rather better deal, and I find that organically-grown vegetables, whilst not always looking so perfectly manicured as the mass-produced alternatives, can have infinitely better flavour. However, don't be too rigid in your criteria, as frozen peas would be a much better choice than stale organic carrots that have the texture of damp sponge.

The Menu

Deciding what to cook is often a most difficult choice, so begin by making a list of your restrictions: the occasion and type of meal you want – even if you love making soup, it might not be practical for a picnic; the limitations of your kitchen, space and equipment – make sure that not everything you need to cook requires the oven and don't plan on boiling a large chicken if you only have one small saucepan; your knowledge and skills – boning quails is not for first-time cooks. Budget we have already discussed, as well as the importance of finding out if there is anything your guests don't, can't or won't eat. This is difficult to establish if you are feeding a crowd, however, most people who aren't vegetarians will eat poultry and certain fish which is why I have based many of the menus in this book around these ingredients. Save your favourite offal, game or shellfish recipes for small gatherings when you can be sure that they will be appreciated.

If you are entertaining informally in the kitchen, it doesn't really matter if you have to get up from the table occasionally to cook a vegetable or thicken a sauce, but do remember that your guests aren't coming for a cookery lesson; plan the meal so that you don't have to do too much last-minute or any smelly cooking. Certain odours, like deep-frying fish or boiling cauliflower, will not heighten the appetite, whereas bread baking in the oven or fresh coffee being brewed will set the nostrils twitching pleasantly.

If your dining table is in another room, your menu should be planned to allow you to be with your guests as much as possible, also keeping any last-minute jobs to a minimum. The first course is where you can show off your imaginative skills, arranging everything prettily on individual plates. If it is a cold dish, it can be ready on the table just before the guests arrive. Not too soon, however, as you don't want to have to eat mayonnaise with a layer of dust on it! Keep the main course as simple as possible. A traditional roast dinner with all the trimmings requires a lot of last-minute jobs, not the least of which is carving. Vegetables that are overcooked will ruin a meal as much as cold plates for hot food, so a vegetable that doesn't need last-minute cooking will save a lot of worries, but there are times when plain boiled or steamed vegetables are called for. Professional chefs often get over this problem by boiling the vegetables in advance until they are just underdone, then plunging them immediately into cold water to stop the cooking process. A few seconds in boiling water just before serving will heat them through and finish the cooking. Another method is to warm them through over a gentle heat in butter.

The sweet course will also need to be completely ready to serve. If the occasion is formal, a recipe for something cold would be advisable. Save the hot puddings for informal meals with family and close friends. Fresh fruit is always a very acceptable finish to any kind of meal.

Remember that cheese is very rich and filling. If you serve it at the very end of a meal, British fashion, after the pudding, your guests will be tempted to eat more than they really want and end up feeling uncomfortable. I prefer to serve cheese either with fruit instead of a pudding, or French-style, before the sweet course. Good cheese is so delicious that it is a shame to relegate it to the tail end of the meal, when everyone is really too full to appreciate it, so why not elevate it to the beginning of the meal and arrange your first course around it, combining it perhaps with some crisp, fresh salad ingredients.

Don't presume that your guests will bring a bottle. If they are very good friends, of course you can ask them, or if it is that kind of a party you can suggest it on the printed invitation. Always make sure that you have enough in stock in case they don't! Do be careful, though, particularly if you have several guests who have brought wine, to notice who brought what. If someone has gone to the trouble and expense to bring a good bottle of wine, you should serve it as early on in the meal as possible, thanking them again and complimenting them on their choice.

Balance your menu so that you don't end up with three courses full of cream, everything on your plate the same colour or every course the same texture. Begin with the dish you know you want to serve, even if it is a pudding, and work around that. Most people fall into the trap of thinking that a special meal must be very fancy and that every bit must be 'interesting'. Certainly an originally-prepared vegetable would go well with a plain roast, or a simply-fried fish, but with a complex casserole or 'made up' dish, vegetables that are simply steamed or boiled would be much more suitable. Daring to be simple is so difficult, yet often the most uncomplicated things are by far the best. Above all, don't feel guilty if you haven't made absolutely everything yourself. We can't all be expert pastry chefs, and not many of us have the time to make our own pâtés. When the French entertain, they very often only cook a main course, relying on the delicatessen counter for a first course and the patisserie for a pudding. Rather than letting lack of time or energy prevent you from inviting the friends you would so much like to see, stick a free-range chicken in the oven, surrounded by potatoes, make a simple green salad while it cooks and serve a bought ready-made first course and some fruit and cheese or good-quality commercial ice cream to finish off.

The company of the host or hostess should provide as much pleasure as the meal itself, so it is important that you assess available energy as well as your available time. It doesn't matter how much fun you might have had cooking, or how superb the meal might be, if you are so exhausted that you feel more like going to bed than making scintillating conversation, and you haven't left enough time to even take off your apron and run a comb through your hair, you will only make your guests feel guilty that you have worked so hard. Being a good 'entertainer' is like being a good ballet dancer – the strain must never show. So clear the decks of everything in your kitchen, pin up your list, and forget that extra little course you thought you just might need. Above all, allow enough time so that you can wind down before your guests arrive and be able to add that final garnish to yourself as well as your delicious food.

Drinks

I cannot pretend to be an expert on wine, and can only advise you to do as I do and be advised by those who are. There is always lots to read on the subject in magazines and newspapers and good tips to be heard on the television and radio. Don't be intimidated by the subject, and don't be afraid to ask your local wine merchant for an opinion. Many supermarket wines, which are often cheaper and usually good quality, have a printed label on the back of the bottle which not only tells you how sweet, dry, light or robust the contents are, but what kind of food it will complement best. In the end you will only find out what you like by trying different kinds. When you discover something new that pleases you, make a little note of it – it's surprising how quickly one forgets names, particularly if they are foreign!

There are one or two simple rules to follow when pairing wine with food, although rules are made to be broken. On the whole, white wines are best served chilled (although not gum-numbing cold), whilst red wines are best served at room temperature and are best opened about an hour beforehand so that they can 'breathe'. White wines are considered more palatable companions to light food like light meats, poultry, fish and vegetables whereas reds are better suited to stronger flavours such as red meats, game and cheese. Champagne, if you can afford it, seems to go with anything. Ultimately, though, it is entirely up to you, and if you want to drink Coca-Cola with your oysters, brown ale with your fish soup, or accompany your roast pheasant with a glass of sweet, warm Sauternes, then go ahead without any feelings of guilt.

There are lots of other things besides wine to drink with food, and they need not be alcoholic. Mineral waters, both still and sparkling, are becoming increasingly popular and should certainly be offered as an alternative, especially when some of your guests are drivers. Cider is rather an underestimated drink, I feel. A good, well-chilled dry one is very refreshing with a picnic or other al fresco meal. Beer is perfect with many exotic cuisines, where the spiciness of the food would overpower the subtle flavours of a good wine. Tea goes perfectly with Chinese food.

I feel that pre-meal drinks that contain strong spirits should be kept for private consumption, or perhaps for family or close neighbours who have only to fall over the fence to get home. For parties, a glass of good sherry or a martini with soda and ice is more suitable than strong gin and tonics or fancy mixed cocktails. A simple glass of chilled white wine is perfect, as you can continue with it for the first course or throughout the meal. Champagne or sparkling wine mixed with orange juice is always popular, as is kir (white wine or champagne with a dash of creme de cassis). In the summer I like to make fake Pimms, merely topping white wine up with sparkling mineral water and adding lots of ice, pieces of fruit, slices of cucumber and mint or lemon balm leaves. It looks so glamorous, tastes delicious and is not too alcoholic.

It really isn't necessary to serve anything at the end of a meal; traditional liqueurs and brandies are not only very

alcoholic, but are they really digestifs? I do occasionally like a glass of port with some nice cheese, but too much will surely guarantee a filthy head the next morning. I find nowadays that, whilst some people love a good cup of coffee to finish a meal, more and more of my guests prefer a cup of clear tea, which is lighter and more refreshing than coffee. Scented teas like Earl Grey or jasmine, or a herbal tea like camomile are good choices.

When choosing your party drinks, remember that as well as being restricted by budget, you must think of suitability for the occasion. If you are giving a drinks party and only want to serve one beverage, a sparkling white wine will probably please more people than Guinness, and a costly crate of vintage Château Margaux might not be fully appreciated at a Twenty-first barbecue.

THEMES AND VARIATIONS

Some parties will benefit greatly from being planned around a theme, or a variation. A Golden Wedding celebration, for instance, lends itself perfectly to 'theming', from the colour of the flowers and napkins to even possibly the food itself. Fancy dress might be just the thing to get an eighteenth birthday party off with a swing, and a new twist on an old theme might be the variation needed to inject a bit of sparkle into seasonal festivities, like perhaps serving the alternative, lighter Christmas meal I have suggested in the menu section. The older generation, with diets to watch, wouldn't perhaps find the idea of sitting down to an old-fashioned tea too thrilling, but the idea of a cosy feast of comforting sandwiches, followed by an orgy of freshly baked home-made cakes, buns and biscuits would be quite a novelty and probably a real treat to a group of healthy, hungry students. What fun to set an old-fashioned table and play suitable music to further conjure up an atmosphere of a time when such leisurely meals were more popular.

Children's parties are perfect occasions for letting your imagination run riot, as ideas, novelties and constant entertainment are almost more important than the food. Children are great socialites and followers of fashion, so if you can give your offspring a party which is a bit different, you will score pretty high points. Having no children of my own, I did quite a bit of market research on the subject and I would advise you to do the same. Children have strong views on the matter and clear likes and dislikes, so it's best to consult with the child in question, rather than plan what you think is a fabulous surprise only to have your efforts greeted with a groan and be told that Jason's mother did that two years ago or that trips to safari parks are quite passé.

The following are what I managed to establish through close consultation with my young advisors, however fashions might have changed by the time you read this. Firstly, that eight-year-olds do not like the same things as six-year-olds or even seven-year-olds. Secondly, that just doing jolly food and arranging a few games isn't enough, but that there should be some other major amusement. This could be a hired entertainer for younger children, but Max, who is eight and a pretty experienced party-goer, told me that the most popular parties involve 'doing something', like going swimming or canoeing, visiting a museum, a trip to the circus or pleasure park or even a trip to the cinema. He voted the idea of theme parties – pirate, outer space, horror – as being *great*, but he was adamant that the guests should have the option of dressing up or not. 'If you tell them they must, they won't want to, but if you tell them they don't have to, they will all want to,' he explained carefully.

Food seems to be secondary, but still very important, and tastes are reasonably similar with all children. Crisps or snacks like healthy sticks of celery or carrot are a 'must' to nibble on before the serious sit-down food begins. Then it seems that savoury food is most important, which can be quite spicy, particularly for older children. Knives and forks are not really the thing, though, and finger food like chicken drumsticks are most popular. Healthy food or junk food seems equally acceptable, so you can make the decision between time-saving frozen burgers or home-made bread and vegetable kebabs. Jelly and ice cream are ever-popular sweet offerings. Don't expect to be complimented on your cooking skills if you serve home-made ice cream, as ice cream is ice cream to kids, and it is easy to buy good quality products with the minimum junk added. Small bowls of sweets and the like scattered about the tables are also a necessary addition.

Any attempts at unusual food presentation will be greatly appreciated. Small children love biscuits or little cakes with their initials on the top, but a group of biggish boys enjoying a monster party might be very impressed with blue spaghetti or green mashed potato, and a cake fashioned into a giant black hairy spider or an open dustbin with fish bones and the like.

I will skim over the business of the cake, as there are so many excellent books available which specialise on the subject in great depth. Small children will be quite happy with a cake baked in a 3- or 4-shaped tin, but if you really can't face the thought of struggling with something complicated, turn to the Yellow Pages and find a professional who will relieve you of your worries and provide your spaceship or Care Bear creation.

Lastly, if you are brave enough to throw a kids' party and don't opt for a trip to MacDonald's, you will need lots of energy and as much help as you can muster. If there are adults at the party, either helping, or just accompanying smaller children, they will probably appreciate a little something to nibble on and a drink of something stronger than Pepsi.

Very special occasions are undoubtedly made even more memorable by planning around a theme. Sometimes this can also make difficult decision-making a much easier task. If you are planning a wedding celebration with a Victorian theme, it will immediately make the choice of the dress for the bride and the type of clothes for the bridesmaids and pages much easier to decide on. Wedding celebrations are occasions when you simply can't overdo things, and nothing can ever be too fancy or too posh; that is, unless you decide on simplicity, in which case a naive rustic theme could be enchanting. If you choose an idea like a Victorian theme, don't feel you must stick to it too rigidly; just go for a feeling and an atmosphere. The bride isn't going to corset herself into a Scarlett O'Hara-size waistline, and nobody's going to worry that it's historically incorrect to use powdered gelatine in the pudding or nylon lace for the tablecloth. It's enough that the table looks pretty and busy and the flowers look romantic and old-fashioned. Museums and books will provide you with plenty of inspiration. It might be fun to adapt some recipes from nineteenth-century cookbooks like Mrs Beeton's for the meal, but again you can't be too literal as tastes in food have changed considerably, and our Victorian ancestors got through what would now seem like horrific quantities. The food should, however, to give the period feel, look rather grand and formal and much attention must be paid to presentation and garnish, and remember when deciding on the design of the cake to follow the theme with a pretty, romantic and rather fussy decoration. Quiet nineteenth-century romantic ballet music playing discreetly in the background when the guests arrive would give a perfect final touch to the Victorian atmosphere.

SETTING THE SCENE
Props

Entertaining is about much more than food, as I have already mentioned, and in your own 'productions' the set is terribly important. Nobody wants to eat bad food off exquisite porcelain, but likewise, no one is going to enjoy your food, no matter how delicious, if they feel as if they're sitting in a junk yard. Organisation again is the key, as well as getting your priorities right. People live busier and busier lives and, although if you were having a member of the Royal Family to stay, I would understand you wanting to wash the nets, if you are simply having the boss and his wife to dinner, it really isn't necessary to spring-clean the entire house. What is important is that the rooms in which your guests will be entertained are clean (or at least look clean), free of ironing boards, Wellington boots and nappy buckets. Most of all, the table should be set and look as attractive as possible before they arrive. Even if you are terribly behind with the food, if the table looks lovely, your guests will feel that they are expected and wanted; as long as they are given a drink and someone to talk to, they won't notice your kitchen panic.

If you have plenty of money, making your table look stunning will be no trouble at all, as there is such a wealth of beautiful things to buy from all over the world, but setting an attractive table need not cost very much at all. The standard of design and the quality of merchandise in the cheaper chain stores is now so good that there is plenty of choice of tableware at very reasonable

prices, and junk shops, charity shops, jumble sales and the like will yield countless second-hand treasures if you really hunt seriously. Things don't have to match, and single plates, glasses or even knives and forks can often be picked up for next to nothing. You will soon collect a 'set' which will be charming, personal and a conversation piece. If you decide to collect plates with a pattern, look for ones with a border, rather than an all-over design, as most food looks better against a plain white or cream background (although sweets and puddings somehow look fine on flowery busy designs). If you are planning to buy your first set of plates new, I would advise choosing the plainest white plates you can find, as these are the most versatile, and will fit in with so many different 'looks' for your table setting.

Tablecloths and coverings will instantly transform your setting, help create a theme or mood, and need not be costly. I have a large collection of cloths which I use to ring the changes, made from lengths of cheap dress fabric, either quickly hemmed on a sewing machine or just frayed all the way round the edges. Pretty napkins can be made in the same way, cost next to nothing and are so much nicer than paper ones. Again, pretty second-hand cloths and napkins can be picked up very cheaply, and no one will mind that the design on each of your beautiful starched white damask napkins is different.

When looking for original ideas and bargains, it is important to keep both your eyes and your mind open – props for your set may come in many disguises. A single chintz curtain or an old shawl or bed cover could make a stunning tablecloth, and an old bedroom jug minus its bowl might make a fabulous vase for a table centrepiece or even an ice 'bucket' for chilling wine. Be brave when setting the table – a dramatic flourish will be

noticed and enjoyed far more than discreet good taste.

Don't be afraid to be extravagant when setting the scene for your entertainment. Remember it's only for one occasion, so mistakes, occasional lapses into bad taste, or merely the amusing won't have lasting consequence. It's not like decorating a room, or choosing new curtains that you are going to have to live with for a long time. It can be such fun to attempt to make the table look different every time you entertain, particularly if you see the same set of friends with regularity. Imagination is all that is needed.

A good tip to remember when designing your 'set' is that, like clothes, a table setting that is suitable for an evening atmosphere with low lights and candles won't look right for a garden party. Drama is called for at night – glowing fabrics, rich colours and glitter, whereas a much simpler, fresher look is more suitable for daylight. Gold cutlery set on a shimmering brocade shawl might look fabulous and give the right dramatic flourish to a late-night supper after the theatre, but could look cheap and tawdry in the bright light of day. Flimsy white gauze and tiny, individual posies of primroses in white egg cups might look entrancing for an Easter lunch, yet limp and insipid after dark.

Sound and Light

Lighting is all-important in setting the scene, as bright, harsh lighting will do nothing for your 'set', and even less for your guests. Dimmer switches are the perfect solution. Candles always add a touch of magic and are flattering to table, food and faces, but remember your guests will want to see what they are eating. Also, don't forget that a mass of candles will give off a considerable amount of heat, particularly on warm evenings.

Unless you are having a disco, or dancing is part of your plan, be very careful about background music – loud Wagner or Iron Maiden will not be a stimulant to dinner-party conversation. On the other hand, a bit of quiet Astrid Gilberto as your guests sip their sangria might set the mood perfectly for your sultry Mexican dinner party.

The Flower Show

Flowers always add the perfect finishing touch. Some people have a knack and can make anything look good. If you aren't one of those people, try to be simple and dramatic. If daffodils are cheap, buy as many as you can afford and just jam them in a mass into a big straight-sided plain glass vase so that the stems show; they will look sensational. Splash out on one really exotic bloom – a great white lily or a bird of paradise – and place it in solitary splendour in the middle of your table, or fill lots of tiny glasses or vases with just one or two small flowers or even a few wild grasses and place them all over the table, perhaps with lots of small 'night light' candles in the spaces. One of the best and quickest ways to use flowers to really spectacular effect, even if you have about as much artistic flair as a rolling pin, is simply to scatter small flower heads or petals at random all over a white cloth. They will stay fresh during the time you are at the table and the effect will gain you much praise for your taste and originality.

Some of you, like me, will be happy to fiddle with flowers for hours, wiring blooms onto rope for stunning swags or carefully poking dandelion heads into a little block of foam to make a row of brilliant cushions of sunshine to march down the centre of a table, so go ahead and enjoy yourself and give your guests the pleasure of your talents. Again, don't be afraid to go over the top a bit – a subtle little Japanese number with two acorns, a bit of driftwood and a single tulip might be just the job for an intimate dinner 'à deux', but will merely look soppy and lost at a larger gathering.

Not everybody has a garden to supply them with flowers for the table whenever they want and florists' flowers, particularly in winter, can be expensive, but 'flowers' can be made from anything, so use a bit of lateral thinking. Of course it is wrong to pick rare wild flowers – if you pick the bluebells which look so stunning carpeting the wood, your bunch will be dead by the time you get them home and your act of vandalism will only sadden the fairies. When the hedgerows are overflowing with cow parsley, though, you can decorate your table with a vase of beautiful creamy lace, and even city 'weeds' can look superb. So look again – perhaps those dandelions or white deadnettles which make you curse so much when they pop up in your garden aren't such a nuisance after all. A friend in Australia was walking home one day before giving a party in the evening to find that the City Council had been pruning trees. He dragged home several 10-foot branches and arranged them around the walls of the room. The effect, as you can imagine, was stunning, and the enchanted guests spent a really special evening in a forest. This friend also demonstrated to me that an 'arrangement' for the table does not have to be just flowers or plants. His menu included a lobster, the head and claws of which soon graced the centre of the table where it emerged from a huge white shell, surrounded by a foam of white gypsophila.

Finishing Touches

The art of serving food needs a book to itself and there simply isn't the room here, so I suggest you apply the same rules to food presentation that I have advised for your floral masterpieces. If

Anything that will hold water can become a vase, and often very effectively – an old teapot which has lost its lid, a decorative tin box, or even a pretty jam jar. However, if you are buying new vases, plain ones will prove to be the most versatile. I love glass vases, as I love to see the stems of flowers. However, flowers like tulips and daffodils are best for this treatment, rather than flowers with woody stems like chrysanthemums which tend to make the water discoloured and slimy-looking after a couple of days.

you have a strong visual sense and don't mind (more to the point, have time for) fiddling around with your *salade composée* plates for the first course, your guests will be very impressed and delighted with their individual art work in food. If, however, your talents are definitely more culinary than artistic, just make your food look as uncluttered and appetising as possible. Although food must look appetising and attractive, its flavour and quality must come first. If you want to arrange individual plates, the first course or even the pudding is the place to perform because you can do your creative tinkering ahead of time. It is unlikely that without a very speedy and efficient partner, you will have time to arrange the main course on individual plates. It's no good it looking spectacular if your vegetables have gone limp and the sauce congeals on cold plates.

If in doubt, keep it simple and remember that not everything has to be garnished. The garnish should be appropriate and edible, so whereas some orange nasturtium flowers might add a brilliant touch to the appearance of your plain green salad, they might also add a pleasant peppery taste to liven it up. The flavour of parsley is very distinctive, and although delicious, is not sympathetic or necessary to all dishes, and that little green sprinkling over everything can make your food both look and taste monotonous.

When serving a hot sit-down dinner, it is advisable to place the food in serving dishes on the table for guests to help themselves, or on a side table or heated trolley (if you are lucky enough to have one) for you to serve them. Your decorative serving dishes and the good-looking fresh food will make the meal attractive. If you are catering for large numbers, particularly cold buffets, some things like puddings are better if you can make them in individual portions, as nothing looks more unattractive and unappetising than an elaborately decorated gâteau or fancy trifle once it has been half-demolished. The photographs in this book will give you some ideas about how to make your food look attractive and appealing, but you can get lots of other good ideas from the excellent food photography which abounds in magazines and books.

One final word: although certain items such as wedding cakes call for elaborate presentation, simplicity is generally the best rule to follow. If in doubt, leave it out, and if you find you have been spending longer than about a minute arranging food on a plate, you are doing something wrong.

Now on to the supporting cast of your production: the food . . .

The Menus

Oriental Cocktail Party

Spicy Fish in Spinach Leaves
Deep-fried Prawns in Coconut Batter
Five-spice Pork-wrapped Quail Eggs
Coriander Lamb in Filo Packets
Chicken Satay
Water Chestnuts in Crispy Bacon

A SELECTION of really special bite-sized treats with an Oriental theme, to serve as hot snacks before lunch or dinner or for a larger drinks party. People always eat more than you expect (particularly when the food is good!) so these quantities make enough for 6 people with hearty appetites to have 12 'bites' each. If a large meal is to follow, 6 'bites' per person would probably be enough, so these would be enough for 12 guests. For a larger party, just increase the ingredients as required. To make your variety of 'bites' even wider, add a few of the excellent Chinese dim sum snacks, now available frozen in some supermarkets and Oriental grocers. They usually just need steaming, frying or heating in the oven for a few minutes, but the cooking instructions will be written on the packet.

Opposite: Spicy Fish in Spinach Leaves (*see over*). Look out for odd unusual plates and platters which could be used for serving food. I found this strange Art Deco plate very cheaply in a car boot sale. The leaf shape and distinctive deep pewter glaze give it a very exotic look which seemed the perfect thing for these delicious little spicy fish parcels. The stiff little garnish of chicory leaves adds to the tropical mood.

Spicy Fish in Spinach Leaves

Serves 6

12 medium-sized spinach leaves, thick stems discarded
1 large onion, peeled and very finely chopped
1–2 cloves garlic, peeled and crushed
2.5 ml/½ tsp. ground turmeric
1 cm/½-inch piece fresh root ginger, peeled and very finely chopped
2.5 ml/½ tsp. salt
5 ml/1 tsp. chilli powder
7.5 ml/1 ½ tsp. ground coriander
7.5 ml/1 ½ tsp. ground cumin
15 ml/1 tbsp. vegetable oil
225 g/8 oz. white fish fillets, skin removed, cut into very small dice

1. Blanch the spinach leaves by boiling them in salted water for 1–2 minutes or until tender. Carefully remove the leaves from the pan with a slotted spoon and plunge into ice water to set the colour. Lay the leaves out flat to dry on a tea towel.
2. Gently fry the onion, garlic and all the spices in the oil for 2–3 minutes, then mix together with the diced fish.
3. Place about 2 teaspoonsful of the fish mixture on the wider end of each leaf. Fold the bottom third of the leaf up, fold the sides in, then roll up into a neat bundle and secure with a toothpick. Arrange the bundles on a lightly oiled plate in a steamer and steam over boiling water for 15–20 minutes. Serve hot.

NOTE: Spinach leaves should ideally be about 12.5 cm/5 inches long, or cut squares approximately that size from larger leaves. If spinach is unavailable, large leaves from firm lettuces like cos can be used successfully instead.

Deep-fried Prawns in Coconut Batter

Makes 12

85 g/3 oz. plain flour
45 ml/3 tbsp. cornflour
5 ml/1 tsp. baking powder
2.5 ml/ ½ tsp. salt
150 ml/5 fl. oz. water (more if needed)
15 ml/1 tbsp. vegetable oil
30 ml/2 tbsp. desiccated coconut
12 large raw prawns, shelled, except for tails, and de-veined
oil for deep frying

Sauce:

60 ml/4 tbsp. coconut milk (see note)
30 ml/2 tbsp. chilli-ginger sauce (see note)

1. In a medium-sized bowl, combine all the dry ingredients except the coconut. Slowly whisk in the water to make a smooth batter, then whisk in the oil and the coconut. Leave the batter to sit for 1 hour.
2. Make the sauce by stirring together the coconut milk and the chilli sauce. Chill 1 hour to let the flavours blend.
3. Pour oil into a heavy-bottomed saucepan or deep-fryer to a depth of 2.5 cm/1 inch. Heat until very hot, but not smoking. Dip each prawn in batter and carefully drop into the oil. Fry for 1–2 minutes, or until batter is golden-brown. Drain on kitchen paper and serve immediately with dipping sauce.

NOTE: Chilli-ginger sauce is available in bottles from large supermarkets, Oriental grocers and specialist food shops.
NOTE: Coconut milk is not the clear juice from inside the nut, but a creamy white liquid which is available in cans or in powdered form to be reconstituted by adding water. It is usually available from

Oriental grocers and some super-markets, but if you can't find it, soak 170 g/6 oz. desiccated coconut in 850 ml/1½ pints boiling water for 30 minutes. Pour it through a sieve, pressing hard to extract as much liquid as possible. This should produce about 600 ml/1 pint coconut milk.

Five-spice Pork-wrapped Quail Eggs

Makes 12

1 dozen fresh quail eggs
170 g/6 oz. minced pork (see note)
2 small spring onions, trimmed and finely chopped
5 ml/1 tsp. five-spice powder (see note)
salt and freshly ground black pepper
2 eggs, beaten
60 g/2 oz. dry white breadcrumbs
oil for deep frying

1. Put the quail eggs in a saucepan with water to cover and bring to the boil. Boil gently for 3 minutes, remove from the heat and put under running water for 1–2 minutes. Leave to cool, then peel off the shells.

2. In a small bowl, combine the pork, chopped onion, five-spice powder and salt and pepper. Beat with a wooden spoon for 1 minute. To coat the eggs, put about 2 heaped teaspoons of pork mix-ture in the palm of your hand and flatten it out to form an oval. Lay an egg in the centre and wrap the meat around it, pinching and pressing to mould the meat completely around the egg.

3. Dip each coated quail egg in the beaten egg and then roll in breadcrumbs to coat completely. Pour oil into a heavy-bottomed saucepan or deep-fryer to a depth of 2.5 cm/1 inch. Heat the oil until very hot, but not smoking, and fry the eggs until golden-brown and crisp all over, 3–4 minutes. Drain on kitchen paper. These are good served hot or cold. They look pretty sliced in half to show the egg and make 'daintier' bites.

NOTE: If you cannot find pork ready-minced, make it yourself using streaky belly pork in a food processor or mincer. The meat should be rather fatty.

NOTE: Five-spice powder is available from large supermarkets, Oriental gro-cers and specialist food shops.

Coriander Lamb in Filo Packets

Makes 12

170 g/6 oz. minced lamb
5 ml/1 tsp. ground cumin
½ large onion, peeled and finely chopped
1 clove garlic, peeled and crushed
15 ml/1 tbsp. finely chopped fresh coriander (see note)
2.5 ml/ ½ tsp. salt
freshly ground black pepper
15 g/1/2 oz. butter, melted
3 sheets filo pastry (see note)
30 g/1 oz. butter, melted

Sauce:

¼ cucumber, peeled and cut in cubes
60 ml/4 tbsp. plain yogurt
1 clove garlic, peeled and crushed
15 ml/1 tbsp. fresh coriander or parsley
salt and freshly ground pepper

1. Preheat the oven to 200°C/gas mark 6. In a bowl, combine the lamb, cumin, onion, garlic, coriander, salt, pepper and melted butter. Stir with a wooden spoon until well mixed.

2. Lay out a sheet of filo pastry and brush with melted butter. Cut lengthways into 4 strips. Place about 2 teaspoonsful of filling in one corner of the pastry and fold over the edge to make a triangle, bringing the corner up to meet the opposite side. Continue folding up the pastry in this manner to form a neat triangular packet. Brush the folded packets with more butter, put them on a baking tray and bake in the pre-heated oven for 18–20 minutes, until golden-brown and crisp.

3. For the sauce, combine all ingredients in a food processor or liquidiser and work until smooth.

NOTE: Fresh coriander makes this recipe very special, but if you cannot find it, use fresh mint, or fresh parsley with a pinch of dried mint.

NOTE: Filo pastry is available fresh or frozen in packages from large supermarkets and continental delicatessens.

How to fold the filo strips to make the Coriander Lamb in Filo Packets.

Chicken Satay

Serves 6

170 g/6 oz. boneless, skinless chicken breast (two average breasts), cut into 24 small cubes
Marinade:
15 ml/1 tbsp. oil
10 ml/2 tsp. soy sauce
10 ml/2 tsp. lemon juice

Sauce:

15 ml/1 tbsp. oil
3 spring onions, trimmed and finely chopped
2 cloves garlic, peeled and crushed
5 ml/1 tsp. ground coriander
2.5 ml/ ½ tsp. ground cumin
2.5 ml/ ½ tsp. ground fennel
2.5 ml/ ½ tsp. chilli powder
1.25ml/ ¼ tsp. cayenne pepper
85g/3oz. peanut butter
150ml/4fl. oz. coconut milk (see p. 30)
15ml/1tbsp. soy sauce
juice of 1 lime
5ml/1tsp. sugar
salt to taste

1. Put the chicken in a shallow bowl with the marinade ingredients, cover with clingfilm and leave to marinate for 1–2 hours.
2. For the sauce, in a small saucepan, heat the oil and cook the spring onions, garlic and all the spices for 2–3 minutes. Add the peanut butter, coconut milk, soy sauce, lime juice, sugar and salt and stir to combine. Taste for seasoning and then process in a food processor or liquidiser until smooth. If the sauce is too thick, thin with a little more coconut milk. Return to the pan to reheat for serving.
3. Skewer the chicken cubes onto wooden toothpicks (soaked in water for 30 minutes) or mini kebab skewers, then grill for 2–3 minutes on each side. Serve hot with satay sauce in a bowl for dipping.

NOTE: The recipe for the sauce produces quite a large amount, but as it is so delicious, it's good to have some extra in the fridge, to add a special touch to some plain grilled meat another day.

Water Chestnuts in Crispy Bacon

Makes 12

200g/7oz. smoked streaky bacon
225g/8oz. tinned water chestnuts, drained

1. Using the back of a knife, scrape each rasher of bacon to stretch it a little and cut into 2 even lengths. Wrap each water chestnut with a length of bacon and secure with a wooden toothpick.
2. Grill for 5–7 minutes until bacon is crispy, and serve immediately.

NOTE: Water chestnuts are available in tins from large supermarkets, Oriental grocers and specialist food shops.

Vegetarian Lunch, Italian Style

Caponata
Salad of Scorched Peppers,
Fennel and Black Olives
Mushroom and Three-cheese Lasagne
Zabaglione Mousse

THE ITALIANS cook so many wonderful dishes that contain no meat or fish, but that are not intentionally vegetarian. This colourful and tasty menu will satisfy vegetarian tastes and be relished equally by non-vegetarians, who won't even notice they are feasting on fleshless fare! I have eaten superb food on several trips to Sicily and it is this beautiful, sunny island that has provided the inspiration for the caponata and the zabaglione mousse, which is flavoured with Sicily's well-loved sweet Marsala wine.

The quantities are intended for 6 people at a sit-down meal, but the menu is carefully planned so that the recipes can be simply expanded to provide an easy-to-prepare buffet for any number of people.

Caponata

Serves 6

675 g/1½ lb. aubergines, wiped and cut into 2.5-cm/1-inch cubes
salt
60 ml/4 tbsp. olive oil
4 celery stalks, cut in 1-cm/½-inch lengths
1 large onion, peeled and roughly chopped
45 ml/3 tbsp. sugar
75 ml/5 tbsp. red wine vinegar
1 × 395 g/14 oz. tin Italian tomatoes, drained
30 ml/2 tbsp. concentrated tomato purée
115 g/4 oz. large green olives, stoned
60 g/2 oz. tin anchovy fillets, well drained, and mashed to a pulp (omit if strictly vegetarian)
20 ml/½ tbsp. sultanas
20 ml/1½ tbsp. capers
freshly ground black pepper
30 g/1 oz. pine nuts (optional)
flat-leaved parsley to garnish

1. Place the aubergine cubes in a colander, sprinkle generously with salt and leave over a sink for 1 hour. Rinse well under cold running water and dry with a tea towel or salad spinner.

2. Heat half the oil in a large frying pan or wok. Cook the celery over a medium heat, stirring often, for 10 minutes. Add the onion and continue to cook for about 10 minutes, stirring frequently, until the onion is soft and golden.

3. Remove the cooked vegetables with a slotted spoon and transfer to a bowl. Heat the remaining oil in the pan and cook the aubergine cubes over a medium heat, stirring frequently for 8–10 minutes until golden. Return the celery and onion to the pan.

4. Mix the sugar and vinegar and add to the pan along with the tomatoes, tomato purée, olives, anchovy fillets, if used, sultanas and capers, and season to taste with salt and pepper. Bring to the boil, reduce the heat and simmer, stirring frequently, for 15 minutes. Add the pine nuts, if used.

5. Transfer the caponata to a serving dish and chill until ready to use, at least 2 hours. Garnish with chopped parsley.

Salad of Scorched Peppers, Fennel and Black Olives

Serves 6

3 red peppers, cored, seeded, and cut into 2.5-cm/1-inch strips
1 bulb fennel, trimmed and sliced into 0.5-cm/¼-inch slices
18 black olives
salt and freshly ground black pepper

1. Heat the grill. Place the pepper strips, skin side up, on a baking tray. Grill close to the heat for about 10 minutes or until the skin is completely black and scorched. Put the peppers in a plastic bag and let rest 5 minutes, then under running water peel off the scorched skin. Dry on kitchen paper.

2. On a serving platter, arrange the skinned peppers, fennel slices and olives.

NOTE: This delicious salad needs no dressing, and is best just as it is with no more than a seasoning of salt and pepper.

Mushroom and Three-cheese Lasagne

Serves 6

1 medium-sized onion, peeled and finely chopped
85 g/3 oz. butter
85 g/3 oz. flour
900 ml/1½ pints milk
340 g/12 oz. gorgonzola cheese, crumbled
340 g/12 oz. cheddar cheese, grated
salt and freshly ground black pepper
freshly grated nutmeg
30 ml/2 tbsp. olive oil
1 large onion, peeled and thinly sliced
1.4 kg/3 lb. mushrooms, wiped and finely chopped
4 cloves garlic, peeled and crushed
5 ml/1 tsp. dried oregano or 10 ml/2 tsp. fresh
3 × 395 g/14 oz. cans Italian tomatoes
85 g/3 oz. freshly grated parmesan cheese
18 pre-cooked lasagne noodles (see note)

1. In a medium-sized saucepan, cook the onions in the butter for 5 minutes until they are soft and transparent. Add the flour and cook for 3–4 minutes, stirring constantly with a wooden spoon. Add the milk, whisking vigorously to prevent lumps. Bring the mixture to the boil, then remove from the heat and add the gorgonzola and the cheddar cheeses and stir until they are melted. Strain the sauce through a sieve and season to taste with salt, pepper and nutmeg.

2. Cook the sliced onions in the olive oil about 5 minutes until soft and transparent, then add the mushrooms and cook until all the liquid rendered from them is evaporated, about 10–15 minutes. Add the garlic, oregano and tomatoes and

continue cooking until the juice has evaporated and the mixture is quite dry, 8–10 further minutes. Season to taste with salt and pepper.

3. Preheat the oven to 180°C/gas mark 4. To assemble the lasagne, spread a thin layer of the cheese sauce in the bottom of an oiled 23 × 30-cm/9 × 12-inch shallow ovenproof dish. Arrange strips of lasagne to cover the bottom of the dish, then coat with about ⅓ of the cheese sauce. Sprinkle over ⅓ of the parmesan cheese, then spread ½ of the mushroom mixture in an even layer. Arrange another layer of lasagne and repeat with another ⅓ of the cheese sauce, parmesan cheese and the remaining mushrooms. Finish with a layer of lasagne, the remaining cheese sauce and the remaining parmesan cheese.

4. Bake in the preheated oven for 40 to 50 minutes, until the sauce is bubbling and brown. Serve on hot plates.

NOTE: Pre-cooked lasagne noodles are now widely available and do not need softening in boiling water before layering with the sauces. However, if you can only find the traditional kind, boil, drain and dry first according to the instructions on the packet.

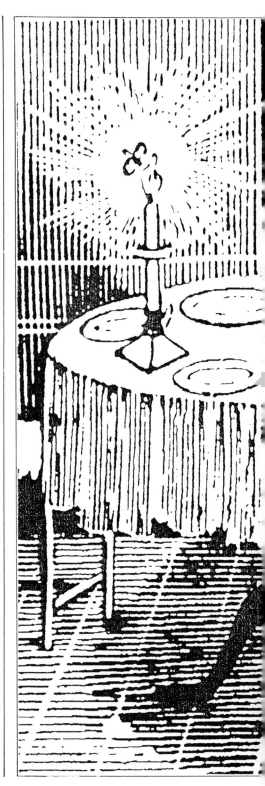

Zabaglione Mousse

Serves 6

8 egg yolks
140 g/5 oz. caster sugar
270 ml/9 fl. oz. drug Marsala wine
1 sachet powdered gelatine
300 ml/½ pint double cream
freshly grated nutmeg to garnish

1. In the top of a double boiler (or a heat-proof bowl set in a saucepan), beat the egg yolks until light and creamy. Over simmering (but not boiling) water, continue beating, gradually adding the sugar. When the yolks have doubled in volume, gradually add all but 60 ml/ 4 tbsp. of the Marsala. Continue beating for 15 minutes, until the mixture is very light and fluffy.

2. Dissolve the gelatine in the reserved Marsala according to the instructions on the packet. Combine it with the zabaglione mixture. Whip the cream until it forms soft peaks and carefully fold into the zabaglione. Pour into an attractive glass bowl or individual glasses and chill until set, at least 2 hours.

3. To serve, sprinkle the top of the mousse with a little grated nutmeg.

NOTE: Marsala is a sweet fortified wine from Sicily and is available from all good wine shops and large supermarkets.

Al Fresco Feast

**Spinach and Ham Roulade
Poacher's Pasties
Coeur à la Crème with Fresh Berries**

Opposite: Spinach and Ham Roulade (*see over*). How pleasant it is, if the weather permits, to eat outside, even if it is in a tiny London back garden. Somehow everything tastes much better. Not for me, though, if the food is served on paper plates, which tend to flop, spill and make things difficult. It's so much more of a treat, also, on a picnic, not to have paper napkins. Pretty flowered ones cost little to make from cheap remnants of dress fabric and are quick and easy to launder.

THE WORD 'picnic' can conjure up scenes of miserable meals eaten cramped in a steamed-up car watching the rain beat down on a leaden sea. Or lunchtimes spent huddling in thick sweaters on a windswept beach eating soggy sandwiches washed down with lukewarm flask coffee.

But let us put aside such dreary thoughts and turn our minds optimistically to the sort of outdoor meal more fitting to Glyndebourne, Henley or just friendly cricket matches on sunny English village greens.

Fill the icebox with chilled champagne or the like and pack your hamper with this upper-class little picnic. Even if the weather doesn't oblige, at least the food will be good!

41

Spinach and Ham Roulade

Serves 6

570 g/1 ¼ lb. frozen spinach (2 10 oz. packages), thawed
30 g/1 oz. butter, melted
freshly grated nutmeg
5 egg yolks, beaten
salt and freshly ground black pepper
5 egg whites, stiffly beaten
225 g/8 oz. smoked ham
30 g/1 oz. softened butter
30 ml/2 tbsp. mayonnaise
7.5 ml/1 ½ tsp. mustard powder
2–3 ripe tomatoes, cut in wedges

Vinaigrette Dressing:

15 m/1 tbsp. lemon juice
45 ml/3 tbsp. olive oil, or half olive oil and half vegetable oil
2.5 ml/ ½ tsp. sugar
1 clove garlic, peeled and crushed (optional)
1.25 ml/ ¼ tsp. mustard powder
2.5 ml/ ½ tsp. salt
1.25 ml/ ¼ tsp. freshly ground black pepper

1. Place all the ingredients for the vinaigrette in a screw-topped jar and shake until amalgamated, or place in a bowl and whisk. Leave at least 1 hour for flavours to develop before using.

2. Heat the oven to 200°C/gas mark 6. Butter a swiss roll tin and line with well-buttered greaseproof paper, snipping the corners to make it fit, and allowing the paper to stand up a little above the edge of the tin.

3. Purée the spinach in a food processor or liquidiser and drain well, squeezing to remove excess liquid.

4. In a large bowl, mix the spinach purée with the melted butter, egg yolks, nutmeg, salt and pepper to taste. Slacken the mixture with a little of the beaten egg white, then carefully fold in the remainder.

5. Gently spoon the mixture into the lined tin, carefully smoothing it into the corners. Bake in the preheated oven on the second to top shelf for 12–15 minutes or until set and slightly browned.

6. Turn the mixture onto a tea towel and cover with another to keep from drying out.

7. To make the filling, finely chop the ham with a knife or in a food processor and mix well with the softened butter, mayonnaise, mustard and salt and pepper to taste.

8. Spread the spinach soufflé with the ham mixture and with the help of a tea towel, roll up lengthways. Leave to cool in the towel.

9. To serve, toss the tomato wedges in the vinaigrette and arrange on 6 individual plates. Cut the roulade into 12 slices and lay 2 slices on each plate with the tomato salad.

NOTE: The vinaigrette recipe can easily be varied to make a whole range of exciting dressings. Try using different oils, such as nut oils, and flavoured vinegars, like raspberry or tarragon, or adding chopped fresh herbs.

Poacher's Pasties

Makes 6

85 g/3 oz. plain flour
salt and freshly ground black pepper
450 g/1 lb. cubed rabbit meat, thawed if frozen
60 ml/4 tbsp. vegetable oil
225 g/8 oz. streaky belly pork, cut into 1 cm/ ½ inch cubes
115 g/4 oz. mushrooms, wiped, left whole if small or sliced if large
225 g/8 oz. leeks, washed and sliced
2 stalks celery, washed and sliced
15 juniper berries, crushed
10 ml/2 tsp. fresh thyme or 5 ml/1 tsp. dried
450 ml/ ¾ pint chicken or vegetable stock
2 quantities shortcrust pastry (see below)
2 egg yolks, beaten

1. Season the flour with salt and pepper. Coat the rabbit cubes with flour and pat to remove any excess; reserve the remaining flour. Heat half the oil in a wok or wide frying pan and fry the pork cubes for 10 minutes. Remove from the pan with a slotted spoon and put into a heavy-bottomed saucepan. In the same frying pan, fry the pieces of rabbit over a medium heat for 10 minutes until completely browned. Remove the rabbit from the pan and put in the saucepan with the pork.

2. To the same frying pan, add the remaining oil and cook the mushrooms, leeks and celery for 5 minutes. Sprinkle over the vegetables 60 g/2 oz. of the reserved seasoned flour and cook for 5 more minutes, stirring constantly. Put the vegetables with the rabbit and pork, add the juniper berries, thyme and stock and season with salt and pepper to taste.

Cover the pan and simmer over moderate heat for 1 hour, stirring occasionally, until the rabbit and pork pieces are very tender. Remove from the heat and leave to cool.

3. Roll out the pastry and cut out 6 18-cm/7-inch circles. Put one-sixth of the cooled rabbit mixture on half of each circle of pastry. Brush the edges with the beaten egg yolk and fold over the pastry to form a half-moon shape. Pinch the edges to seal and brush the whole pasty with more egg yolk. Heat the oven to 200°C/gas mark 6. Chill the pasties in the refrigerator for 30 minutes, then bake in the preheated oven for 30–40 minutes until the pastry is brown and the filling is heated. Leave to cool and serve at room temperature.

Shortcrust (Basic Pie) Pastry

225 g/8 oz. plain flour
3 ml/ ¾ tsp. salt
115 g/4 oz. cold butter, cut into pieces
1 egg yolk, lightly beaten
45 ml/3 tbsp. cold water

1. Place the flour and salt in a mixing bowl and rub in the butter until the mixture resembles fine breadcrumbs.

2. Mix in the egg yolk and water – adding more water if necessary – and, working quickly, bring together the mixture until it forms a smooth dough.

3. Wrap and chill for 30 minutes before rolling out.

NOTE: This can be made in a food processor, but do not overwork.

Coeur à la Crème with Fresh Berries

Serves 6

285 ml/ ½ pint double cream
225 g/8 oz. cream cheese
15 ml/1 tbsp. caster sugar
2 egg whites
450 g/1 lb. soft fruit (choose from strawberries, raspberries, fraises de bois, etc.)

1. In a large bowl, slowly stir the cream into the cream cheese. Add the sugar and combine well.

2. Beat the egg whites until stiff but not dry and fold carefully into the cheese mixture.

3. Line 6 perforated heart-shaped moulds with damp muslin. Spoon the mixture evenly into the moulds and place on a large plate. (This will catch the liquid that will drain out.) Leave in the refrigerator overnight to drain and chill.

4. To serve, unmould each heart on to a chilled plate and surround with fruit.

Old-fashioned Afternoon Tea

Salmon and Cucumber Sandwiches on Brown Bread
Egg and Cress Sandwiches on White Bread
My Mother's Scones with Jam and Cream
Shortbread Biscuits
Mary Whittle's Lemon Cake
Macaroons
Jam Tarts
Chocolate-raspberry Roulade

IT'S SAD THAT Britain's two most successful meals, breakfast and tea, are now becoming almost extinct in their traditional form. With the modern sensible trend towards much healthier eating, afternoon tea – with all the cream, sugar and butter it must contain to be a success – is hardly compatible. Yet what fond childhood memories I have of sitting round a roaring coal fire on a Saturday winter's afternoon, eating hot buttered toast to the hypnotic, and to me, incomprehensible, sing-song rhythm of the football results on the radio, whilst the pikelets were being toasted in front of the flames on the end of an ancient wire toasting fork. So forget healthy diets and spoil yourself occasionally by inviting round some friends to share this delightfully nostalgic afternoon tea.

The menu and quantities given here are for a pretty hearty tea, but you needn't serve all the items – just select your favourites if you want to serve a lighter meal. However, a real teatime 'bash' is great for Sunday afternoons, when you have had a late breakfast and no lunch. I suggest you walk the dog beforehand in order to work up a healthy appetite, or perhaps a walk after tea would be an even better idea!

For the sandwiches, simply mash some drained tinned salmon with a squeeze of lemon and a good twist of black pepper and spread on buttered brown bread with thinly sliced cucumber. For the white sandwiches, mix chopped hard-boiled eggs with a little well-seasoned mayonnaise and some chopped mustard and cress. You should, of course, cut off all the crusts and make a 'dainty' arrangement of the sandwiches on pretty, old-fashioned plates.

My Mother's Scones

Makes 18 5-cm/2-inch scones

140 g/5 oz. soft margarine
340 g/12 oz. self-raising flour
45 g/1 ½ oz. sugar
pinch of salt
1 egg, beaten
85 ml/3 fl. oz. milk
60 g/2 oz. sultanas
Jam and cream to serve

1. Heat the oven to 220°C/gas mark 7. Put the margarine and flour into a medium-sized bowl and, using your fingers, rub the margarine into the flour. Mix in the sugar and salt, then combine the egg and milk and using a fork, and the liquid to the flour and mix just until it makes a soft dough. Alternatively, work the margarine, flour, sugar and salt in a food processor, then transfer to a bowl to add the liquid.

2. Roll the dough on a floured work surface to 2-cm/ ¾-inch thickness and cut out scones using a 5-cm/2-inch pastry cutter.

3. Bake on an oiled baking tray in the middle of the preheated oven for 10–12 minutes, or until risen and lightly browned, but do not overbake. Cool on a wire rack and serve with jam and whipped cream (or clotted if you can get it).

NOTE: It is quite surprising how many different recipes there are for scones. I may be biased, but I find my mother's quite the best. I must apologise to her here for 'tampering' with her original list of ingredients, because, although she adds none, I prefer the recipe with a pinch of salt!

Shortbread Biscuits

Makes 16 biscuits

170 g/6 oz. plain flour
60 g/2 oz. sugar
pinch of salt
115 g/4 oz. butter

1. Heat the oven to 150°C/gas mark 2. Place the flour, sugar, salt and butter in a bowl and with your fingers, rub in the butter until the ingredients form a dough.

2. On a floured work surface, roll out the dough to a 1-cm/ ½ inch thick rectangle, approximately 15 × 20 cm/6 × 8 inches. Using a spatula, carefully transfer the dough to a buttered baking tray. With a sharp knife, trim the edges to form a neat rectangle, then cut the dough into 15 2.5/7.5-cm/1 × 3-inch bars, but do not separate them. Lightly prick the shortbreads with a fork.

3. Bake in the preheated oven for 60 minutes; the shortbreads will be an even blond colour. Let cool on the baking tray a few minutes, then using a knife if necessary, separate along cuts and cool on a wire rack.

NOTE: These are even better if kept for a few days in an airtight container, so make a double batch, as there certainly won't be any left from the first to keep!

Mary Whittle's Lemon Cake

Makes 1 medium loaf

115 g/4 oz. softened margarine
170 g/6 oz. self-raising flour
170 g/6 oz. caster sugar
2 eggs
60 ml /4 tbsp. milk
grated zest and juice of 1 lemon
60 ml/3 heaped tbsp. icing sugar

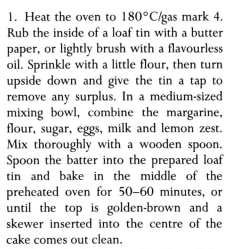

1. Heat the oven to 180°C/gas mark 4. Rub the inside of a loaf tin with a butter paper, or lightly brush with a flavourless oil. Sprinkle with a little flour, then turn upside down and give the tin a tap to remove any surplus. In a medium-sized mixing bowl, combine the margarine, flour, sugar, eggs, milk and lemon zest. Mix thoroughly with a wooden spoon. Spoon the batter into the prepared loaf tin and bake in the middle of the preheated oven for 50–60 minutes, or until the top is golden-brown and a skewer inserted into the centre of the cake comes out clean.

2. With a knife, loosen the edges of the cake from the tin. Mix together the lemon juice and icing sugar and pour evenly over the cake. Leave in the tin until cold, then remove and cut into 1 cm/ ½ inch slices to serve.

NOTE: It is hard to believe that anything that is so quick and simple to make could be as good as this excellent cake.

Macaroons

Makes 12

115 g/4 oz. caster sugar
115 g/4 oz. ground almonds
1 egg
½ quantity shortcrust pastry (see p. 43)

1. Heat the oven to 220°C/gas mark 7. In a small bowl, mix the almonds and sugar with the egg to make a soft paste. Roll out the pastry dough very thinly and line 12 tartlet moulds. With any scraps of dough, cut 24 5-cm/2-inch thin strips to use as decoration. Chill the tartlets and pastry strips for 20 minutes in the refrigerator.
2. Fill each tartlet with 10 ml/2 tsp. of the almond mixture. Lay the strips of pastry dough across top of each to form a cross and pinch the edges to seal. Bake in the preheated oven for 20 minutes until the crust is golden-brown and the filling is slightly puffed.

Jam Tarts

Makes 12

½ quantity shortcrust pastry (see p. 43)
80 ml/4 heaped tbsp. raspberry jam

1. Heat the oven to 220°C/gas mark 7. Roll out the pastry dough very thinly and line 12 tartlet moulds. Chill for 20 minutes in the refrigerator.
2. Fill each mould with 1 heaped teaspoonful of jam, and bake for 15–20 minutes in the preheated oven until the crust is golden-brown.

NOTE: I usually make 6 with one colour jam and 6 with another, or better still, lemon curd. You must use really good jam. I always buy the home-made product when I see it on sale at summer fairs, country bazaars and jumble sales.

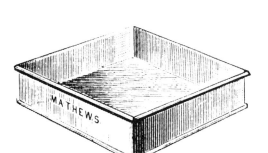

Chocolate-rasberry Roulade

Serves 6

5 eggs, separated
225 g/8 oz. caster sugar
170 g/6 oz. plain chocolate
grated zest and juice of 1 medium orange
140 ml/ ¼ pint double cream
115 g/4 oz. raspberries (fresh or frozen), slightly crushed with a fork
caster sugar for sprinkling

1. Oil a 23 × 30-cm/9 × 13-inch swiss roll tin and line with oiled greaseproof paper, snipping the corners to ensure a perfect fit. Allow the paper to stand up 2.5 cm/1 inch above the sides of the tin.
2. With an electric whisk, beat the egg yolks and sugar to a thick ribbon consistency, about 10 minutes.
3. Heat the oven to 200°C/gas mark 6. Melt the chocolate in a pan with the orange zest and juice over a low heat. Cool and fold into the egg yolk mixture. Beat the egg whites until very stiff. Fold in a quarter of the beaten egg whites to slacken the mixture, then gently but thoroughly fold in the remainder. Pour the mixture into the lined tin, easing it gently into the corners. Bake for about 20–25 minutes in the preheated oven or until the centre feels firm to the touch.

Remove from the oven, cover with a damp tea towel and leave to become quite cold.
3. Whip the cream stiffly, then fold in the raspberries. Chill for 1 hour. Turn the sponge onto a dry tea towel sprinkled with caster sugar. Spread the raspberry cream onto the sponge in an even layer. Roll up the roulade with the tea towel. Chill for at least 1 hour before slicing.

Nouvelle Noel

Warm Smoky Fish Mousse with Grapefruit Salad
Sauternes-poached Quails' Breasts with Stilton Sauce
Vegetable Tartlets
Buttered Chestnuts
Brandied Fruit in Port Wine Jelly

Opposite: Warm Smoky Fish Mousse with Grapefruit Salad (*see over*). My polished oak dining table provides an attractive and warm background for a formal Christmas setting, which relies for its seasonal effect on no more than the red and green ribbon bows which make the napkin rings and the winter arrangement of jolly red berries and evergreens in the fir cone basket.

UNDOUBTEDLY, a well-cooked Christmas dinner with all the traditional trimmings is hard to beat, particularly when feeding a large number of people. Such festive gatherings often include a liberal sprinkling of children and teenagers whose invariably conservative tastes will quickly make them object to any attempt to liven up the turkey stuffing with lychees and pickled Japanese ginger, or a novel idea for serving the pudding in interesting little parcels of Greek pastry . . .

However, should your Christmas feast consist of a small gathering of sophisticated adults who might prefer a lighter, more modern feast, here is a menu that, whilst it retains many of the traditional flavours reminiscent of traditional British Christmas fare, owes much more to the influence of modern French cuisine.

Warm Smoky Fish Mousse with Grapefruit Salad

Serves 6

400 g/14 oz. firm white fish, trimmed of skin and bones
140 g/5 oz. kipper fillets, trimmed of skin and bones
2 egg whites
salt and freshly ground black pepper
freshly grated nutmeg
15 ml/1 tbsp. chopped fresh parsley
390 ml/13 fl. oz. double cream
2 grapefruits, peeled and cut into segments, with the juice reserved
1 head radicchio, washed and leaves separated
1 small head frisée or other bitter greens, washed and leaves separated
1 quantity vinaigrette dressing (see p. 42), made with reserved grapefruit juice instead of lemon juice

1. Combine the white fish, kipper fillets, egg whites, salt, pepper, nutmeg and parsley in a food processor or liquidiser and blend well for 2–3 minutes. Add the cream a little at a time, mixing well after each addition. Pour into buttered individual moulds and chill from 1 to 24 hours.

2. Heat the oven to 190°C/gas mark 5. Put the moulds in a bain-marie, cover with kitchen foil and bake in the preheated oven for 25 minutes, until mousses are just firm to the touch. Leave to cool slightly in the bain-marie for 5–10 minutes.

3. To serve, toss the salad greens with the vinaigrette and arrange on individual plates, leaving space in the centre for the mousses. Divide the grapefruit sections between the plates, then place the warm mousses in the centre.

NOTE: For the salad, it might be more convenient to buy a bag of ready-to-use mixed salad leaves. These are available from many good food shops and supermarkets.

Sauternes-poached Quails' Breasts with Stilton Sauce

Serves 6

12 quails, thawed if frozen
1 small onion, quartered, skin left on
1 small carrot, washed and roughly chopped
1 bay leaf
pinch of thyme
salt and freshly ground black pepper
180 ml/6 fl. oz. Sauternes or other good quality sweet dessert wine
60 g/2 oz. melted butter
140 ml/ ¼ pint chicken stock
140 g/5 oz. Stilton cheese, cut into small bits

1. Carefully cut off the legs and wings of the quails. Reserve the legs and put the wings in a medium-sized saucepan. Remove the skin from the birds and add to the saucepan. Using a very sharp pointed knife, remove both breasts carefully from each bird, slicing either side of the sharp breast bone, and using a gentle sawing motion with the blade of the knife pressed against the rib cage. Reserve the breasts.

2. Add the carcasses to the saucepan with the onion, carrot, bay leaf and thyme and season with a little salt and pepper. Pour over 1.1 litres/2 pints of cold water. Bring to the boil, skimming away any scum as it rises to the surface.

Cover the pan and simmer over a very low heat for 1 hour. Strain through a sieve into a clean pan, discarding the solids. Boil the stock rapidly over a high heat until it reduces to 140 ml/ ¼ pint, and reserve.

3. Very lightly grease the bottom of a saucepan with a little of the melted butter. If possible, use a pan which will just accommodate the breasts in one layer. Sprinkle the breasts with a little salt and pepper and pour over the wine. Brush the legs (these still have the skin on them) on both sides with the remaining melted butter and season with salt and pepper. Arrange in one layer in a grill pan. Heat the grill to high and grill the legs for 5 minutes on each side. Keep warm.

4. Meanwhile, bring the breasts in the wine to the boil. Reduce the heat to low and simmer for no more than 3 minutes. Remove the breasts with a slotted spoon and keep warm on a covered plate. Increase the heat under the pan with the wine in it and reduce to 45 ml/3 tbsp. Put this with the chicken stock and cheese in a liquidiser or food processor and purée to a smooth sauce. Return to the saucepan and reheat gently. Arrange the poached breasts to one side of each large plate. Place the grilled legs on top and spoon over some of the sauce.

NOTE: Removing the quails' breasts is not as difficult as it sounds; it just requires a little care and patience and is well worth the effort.

Vegetable Tartlets

Makes 6

6 cloves
1 large onion, peeled and halved
600 ml/1 pint milk
salt and freshly ground black pepper
115 g/4 oz. fresh white breadcrumbs
75 g/2 ½ oz. butter
6 cooked 10-cm/4-inch individual shortcrust tartlet cases
selection of cooked vegetables, slightly underdone: sliced carrots, asparagus tips, artichoke bottoms, petits pois

1. Stick 3 cloves into each onion half and put in a saucepan with the milk and salt and pepper to taste. Bring to the boil and simmer for 15 minutes. Remove the onion and cloves and stir in the breadcrumbs. Remove from the heat and leave to soak for 30 minutes. Add 60 g/2 oz. of the butter, reheat and simmer gently for 5 minutes.

2. Fill the tartlet cases with the bread sauce and arrange the vegetables attractively on top. To serve, place 2.5 ml/ ½ tsp. butter on top of each and heat through in a moderate oven, approximately 190°C/gas mark 5, for 5 minutes until hot.

NOTE: These unusual tartlets are always such a success with guests that I now occasionally serve them as a starter, surrounded by salad leaves – particularly when entertaining vegetarians.

Buttered Chestnuts

Serves 6

18 cooked, peeled chestnuts, either
roasted or tinned

85 g/3 oz. butter

salt and freshly ground black pepper

1. Heat the chestnuts in a pan with the butter and season to taste with salt and pepper.

NOTE: This is, in fact, much better if you cook the chestnuts yourself, but it is a fiddly job. However, if you live in a city which has 'hot chestnut men' on street corners, you can buy them ready-roasted and save a lot of trouble.

Brandied Fruit in Port Wine Jelly

Serves 6

250 g/9 oz. mixed dried fruit

170 ml/6 fl. oz. brandy

300 ml/ ½ pint port

1 sachet powdered gelatine

1. Marinate the dried fruit in the brandy in a small bowl covered with clingfilm for at least 6 hours or overnight. Drain the fruit in a wire sieve over a measuring jug reserving the brandy. Divide the fruit between 6 small moulds or one large one. Make the brandy up to 480 ml/16 fl. oz. with the port.

2. Dissolve the gelatine in 90 ml/3 fl. oz. of the liquid, according to the instructions on the packet, add to the rest of the liquid and pour over the fruit in the moulds. Refrigerate for at least 6 hours, or until set. To serve, dip the moulds briefly in hot water, dry and turn out the jellies onto plates.

NOTE: I make these in small moulds with round bottoms – little teacups would do – so that they turn out looking like miniature Christmas puddings.

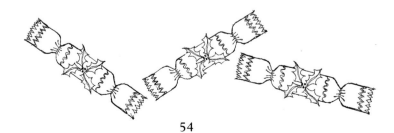

Beginners Please

**Chilled Curried Cauliflower Soup
with Orange-marinated Sultanas
Chicken in Herb and Lemon
Sauce in Pastry Baskets
Carved Pineapple**

ALTHOUGH THIS menu is designed to tempt those with almost no experience into the kitchen to expand their culinary skills, the recipes should please even those who consider themselves gourmets. And after all, even those of us who are experienced cooks occasionally find ourselves lacking in time, energy or inspiration. This menu is an inexpensive, easy and delicious meal with universal appeal.

Chilled Curried Cauliflower Soup with Orange-marinated Sultanas

Serves 6

1 large onion, peeled and chopped
675 g/1½ lbs. cauliflower florets
1.7 litres/3 pints chicken stock (see following recipe)
15–30 ml/1–2 tsp. curry powder (according to taste)
salt and freshly ground black pepper
110 g/4 oz. sultanas
90 ml/3 fl. oz. (about 6 tbsp.) orange juice
a small pot of natural yogurt

1. Put the onion and cauliflower in a large saucepan with the stock and curry powder and season to taste with salt and pepper. Go steady with the seasoning at this stage as your stock should already be well seasoned. Bring to the boil and simmer for 15–20 minutes, or until the vegetables are soft. In a food processor or liquidiser, purée the soup in batches and return to a bowl. Taste for seasoning. Allow to cool, then chill for at least 4 hours in the fridge or overnight. (If you are short of time, an hour or so in the freezer will speed things up.)

2. Meanwhile, put the sultanas in a small bowl and cover with the orange juice. Cover with cling film and leave to macerate in the fridge until required. They are best left at least 4 hours.

3. To serve, divide the soup between 6 cold soup bowls (if you have room in the fridge to chill them, even better). Divide the soaked sultanas between each serving and finish with a blob of yogurt in the centre.

NOTE: If you would like to serve this soup hot, add the soaked sultanas after you have puréed the soup, and reheat.

If you want to make this soup and you do not have home-made stock, look for 'no additive' stock cubes which are now available and don't have that distinctive made-with-a-cube taste, or you can buy an excellent powdered vegetable stock called Swiss Bouillon Powder from health food shops.

Chicken in Herb and Lemon Sauce in Pastry Baskets

Serves 6

1 boiling chicken, about 1.4 kg/3 lb.
2 medium-sized onions, washed, halved, with skin left on
2 medium-sized carrots, washed and roughly chopped
1–2 stalks celery, washed and roughly chopped (optional)
1 bay leaf
1 small bunch parsley (or just the parsley stems)
5-cm/2-inch strip of lemon zest
salt and freshly ground black pepper
6 sheets of frozen ready-rolled puff pastry, thawed (see note on page 58)
1 egg yolk, beaten
40 g/1½ oz. butter
40 g/1½ oz. flour
430 ml/¾ pint stock, made by cooking chicken
430/¾ pint ml milk
juice of 1 lemon
2 spring onions, trimmed and finely chopped (including green part)
15 ml/1 tbsp. fresh parsley, finely chopped
15 ml/1 tbsp. mixed fresh herbs, finely chopped (choose from tarragon, dill, chervil, chives and other mild-flavoured herbs)

1. Put the chicken in a large pot with 3 litres/5 pints water and the onion, carrots, celery, bay leaf, parsley and lemon zest. Season with salt and pepper to taste. Bring the water to the boil; reduce the heat, cover the pot and simmer over a low heat for 1½ hours.

2. Remove the chicken from the liquid and set aside to cool slightly. Strain the stock through a sieve into a bowl and discard the solids. Chill the stock until the fat has solidified on the top – 3–4 hours in the refrigerator or 1–1½ hours in the freezer. Remove the fat with a slotted spoon or fish slice, and either discard or keep for frying other foods.

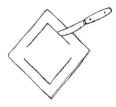

3. To make the pastry baskets, cut the thawed puff pastry into 6 15-cm/6-inch squares. Brush the squares with beaten egg yolk. With a sharp knife, make cuts 2 cm/¾ inch from the edges; in two opposite corners, stop the cuts 3 cm/1¼ inches short of the edge. Bring one cut edge over and place along the opposite inside corner of the square. Press down gently to seal. Repeat with the opposite corner. (See diagram.) Brush the basket again with beaten egg yolk, but take care not to let the yolk run down the side, as this will prevent the pastry rising evenly. Chill until 30 minutes before using.

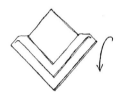

4. Cut the chicken into bite-sized pieces, discarding skin, bone and gristle. Set aside. Carefully remove the fat from the stock and discard. Melt the butter in a heavy-bottomed saucepan over a medium heat. Stir in the flour and milk and cook, stirring constantly with a wooden spoon for 2 minutes. Add the stock, whisking furiously with a wire whisk to prevent lumps forming, then add the milk and continue to whisk. Bring to the boil, reduce the heat and simmer, stirring occasionally for 5 minutes. Stir in the lemon juice, chopped spring onion and the herbs and season well with salt and pepper to taste. Mix in the chicken pieces and cook over a low heat for a few minutes until the chicken is heated through. Keep warm.

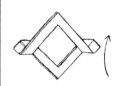

5. Heat the oven to 220°C/gas mark 7. Place the pastry baskets on a dampened baking tray and bake for 15–20 minutes until well-risen and golden-brown. If the centre of the basket has risen a lot, cut some of the pastry away and hollow out the centre with a sharp knife to allow room for the chicken.

6. To serve, place the pastry baskets on 6 individual plates and spoon in the chicken in herb sauce, letting some spill over the sides. Serve with fresh vegetables of your choice.

NOTE: Many supermarkets sell packets of frozen puff pastry, ready-rolled in neat squares. There are normally only 5 squares in each packet, so you will need to buy two packets if you are feeding 6 people. Either let the second packet thaw just enough to let you peel off your sixth square and return the rest to the freezer, or cook all 10 pastry squares and you can then freeze the four spare baskets for use at a later date. (They make an ideal container for any kind of fruit for a delicious instant pudding.) You could, of course, use your own pastry or the variety sold frozen in a block, which you would simply roll out thinly and cut to the required size and shape.

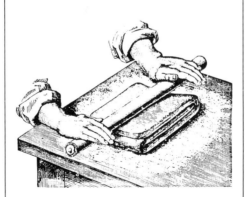

Carved Pineapple

Serves 6–8

1 large ripe pineapple (with the leaves in good condition)
1 punnet of strawberries, or other fruit in season

1. Using a very sharp knife, cut a thin slice off the bottom of the pineapple. This will be the base that the finished pineapple will stand on so make sure it is level at this stage.

2. Cut a small slice off the top to include the leaves and reserve as this will go back on the finished 'carving' as the final garnish.

3. Working from top to bottom, cut away the skin in thin slices.

4. There will be small dark spots all over the fruit. These little hard bits run in diagonal lines, spiralling around the pineapple. Decide whether the clockwise or anti-clockwise lines are the most regular and cut along each side of these with your knife sloping inwards and under the spots. By doing this, you will cut away long triangular sectioned strips which should contain all the hard spots. Discard these. Work carefully all the way round the fruit, being especially careful not to cut away more fruit than you need.

5. Now slice the fruit across into 6 or 8 portions (depending on the size of the fruit), keeping them in order.

6. Now reassemble the 'carved' pineapple in an upright position on a serving plate, carefully matching the spiral grooves. (Don't be put off, this is much simpler to do than it is to describe!) Replace the leafy top and surround with strawberries.

NOTE: When strawberries are not in season, decorate the plate with orange slices or any other fruit you think looks pretty. You can serve this on its own or with cream or vanilla ice cream if you like.

Victorian Wedding

**Jellied Caviare and Soured
Cream Consommé
Salmon Wellington
Berry Charlotte**

EVERY BRIDE, and every bride's mother, wants her wedding to be totally unique and better than any other bride's has ever been before. The dress, the food, the flowers; everything must be perfect and as original as possible. The dress will be far more elaborate than anything she has ever worn before and is ever likely to wear again. The food, the flowers, and in fact everything about the nuptial celebrations, can be pretty fancy too. This is one time when restraint and discreet good taste can be thrown out of the window. When given full licence to plan something which can be so extravagant, it is often difficult to know where to begin. Planning around a theme can help keep a lot of difficult decision-making within bounds. Work around a colour, the season of the year, or even a historical period as with this menu which, although not an authentic Victorian meal (modern tastes would not cope with such gargantuan feasts!), has been adapted from nineteenth-century recipes to fit in with the romantic period theme.

The quantities given are for only 6 people. This is such a delicious menu that it would be also perfect for a small dinner party when you really want to go to town. For a wedding or other big party, simply multiply the ingredients by the required quantity, but remember that the main course requires a certain amount of last-minute preparation and more than one pair of hands would make the speedy presentation of the food on the individual plates much easier to manage.

Salmon Wellington (*see page 65*) photographed in an unashamedly romantic setting. The secret of creating a Victorian atmosphere is to create a table setting with a charming clutter, where nothing should be plain. The crowded glasses (cheap fake 'cut' crystal from a discount hardware shop) add to the glitter and shimmer of the gilded cutlery and the elaborately folded napkins give an air of old-fashioned formality.

The flowers add the final extravagant touch, and are both romantic and formal. The Victorian epergne in the table centre was created by firmly fixing a tall narrow vase on to a china cake stand with Blue Tack. The flowers disguise the fact that they do not match.

The swags are deceptively easy and quick to make. Simply fix the flowers and leaves on to a length of rope with a continuous twist of soft florists wire, tying them at intervals with large bows and fixing the bows to the table cloth with safety pins. Mostly garden flowers were used here – choisia with two shades of pink blossom – but the gypsophila, bought from a florist, adds the perfect foamy, lacy bridal look.

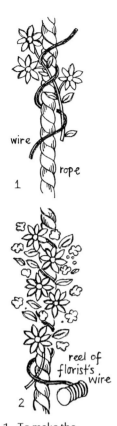

wire

rope

1

reel of
florist's
wire

2

1. To make the flower swags, you will need a piece of pliable rope (about the weight of a skipping rope) which is long enough to go around the table (or along the front of it if it is for a buffet or the 'top table' at a wedding) allowing enough extra length for the swagging. You will also need some soft wire (available on a reel from good florists) and some ribbon for the bows.
2. Separate out all your leaves and sprigs of flowers into piles of each sort.
3. Mark off where the top of each swag will be along the rope with a little bit of

Jellied Caviare and Soured Cream Consommé

Serves 6

1 × 450 ml/15 fl. oz. tin beef consommé
1 sachet powdered gelatine
30 ml/2 tbsp. black lumpfish 'caviare'
30 ml/2 tbsp. water
240 ml/8 fl. oz. double cream, acidulated with 15 ml/1 tbsp. lemon juice
mixed salad greens, including chicory, radicchio, mache
1 quantity vinaigrette dressing (see p. 42)

(see p. 42)

1. Brush the insides of 6 small moulds with vegetable oil, then wipe out thoroughly with kitchen paper – only the faintest trace of oil should remain. Put the consommé in a small saucepan and over a low heat dissolve half the sachet of gelatine, according to the instructions on the packet. (The tinned consommé will be slightly jellied to begin with.)
2. Pour a 1-cm/½-inch layer of consommé in the bottom of each mould and place in the refrigerator until set, about 1 hour. (Leave the remainder of the consommé in a jug at room temperature – you do not want it to set, but if it does, stand the jug in a bowl of warm water.)
3. In a small bowl, mix the caviare with 45 ml/3 tbsp. of the liquid consommé. Place in the fridge until just thickening, but not set. Drop 5 ml/1 tsp. of the caviare mixture neatly into the centre of the jellied consomme in the moulds, trying to keep it away from the edges. Return the moulds to the refrigerator for about 30 minutes until set.
4. When the caviare is set, carefully pour the remaining consommé into the moulds. Chill for another 1–2 hours until set.

5. Meanwhile, dissolve the remaining ½ sachet of gelatine in the 30 ml/2 tbsp. water according to the instructions on the packet. Whip the soured cream until it is slightly fluffy, then add the gelatine and stir well to combine. When the last layer of consommé has just set, spoon in the soured cream and smooth with the back of a spoon to make a flat surface. Chill the moulds for at least 2 more hours, or until ready to serve.
6. To serve, dip the moulds briefly in a bowl of warm water and unmould on to the centre of chilled plates. Toss the salad with the vinaigrette and arrange attractively around the jellied consommé moulds.

Salmon Wellington

Serves 6

85 g/3 oz. smoked salmon
40 g/1½ oz. butter
15 ml/1 tbsp. lemon juice
freshly ground black pepper
1 cucumber, washed
1 quantity puff pastry (see page 66)
1 egg, beaten
18 button mushrooms, wiped and stems trimmed
5 ml/1 tsp. butter
6 salmon steaks, 1.5–2.5 cm/¾–1 inch thick
salt and freshly ground black pepper
180 ml/6 fl. oz. white wine
5 -cm/2-inch strip of lemon zest

Sauce

90 ml/3 fl. oz. lemon juice
85 g/3 oz. butter
freshly snipped chives

1. Combine the smoked salmon, butter, lemon juice and black pepper to taste and work to a paste using a fork or food processor. Set aside.

2. Trim the ends of the cucumber and cut it into 6 even lengths. Cut these pieces into quarters lengthways, then slice off the seeds, parallel to the skin. This will produce rectangles of cucumber approximately 0.5–1 cm/¼–½ inch thick. Round off the corners with a sharp knife to produce a lozenge shape.

3. Heat the oven to 220°C/gas mark 7. Roll out the pastry to a 0.5-cm/¼-inch thickness and stamp out 6 × 10-cm/ 4-inch circles using a pastry cutter. Brush the circles with the beaten egg, transfer to a baking tray and chill for 30 minutes. Bake in the preheated oven for 20 minutes, until risen and golden brown. When cool enough to handle, slice the cooked pastry circles in half horizontally through their equators.

4. Cook the cucumber in gently boiling salted water 8–10 minutes until just tender. Drain and keep warm. Cook the mushrooms in gently boiling salted water with 5 ml/1 tsp. butter for about 5 minutes, until just tender. Keep warm.

5. Place the salmon steaks in a frying pan large enough to hold all 6 in one layer. Sprinkle with salt and pepper, pour over the wine and add enough water to come about halfway up the side of the salmon. Add the lemon zest and cover the pan. Bring just to a boil and simmer gently for 3–5 minutes until the salmon is no longer translucent. Remove from the heat and keep warm.

6. While the salmon is cooking, make the sauce by heating the lemon juice and whisking in the butter a little at a time until it is melted. Add the chives and season with salt and pepper.

7. To serve, place the bottom of a puff pastry round in the middle of a heated plate. Pat the salmon steak dry with kitchen paper and place on top. Spread a little of the smoked salmon butter on the steak, then cover with the other pastry round. Arrange the cucumber and mushroom in an alternating pattern round the plate and pour round a ribbon of sauce.

wire or sticky tape.

4. Starting at the middle, i.e. the lowest point of each swag, twist the end of the reel of wire around the rope to secure it, then begin placing the flowers and leaves in a random fashion along the rope, holding each in place by the stem with a thumb and finger of one hand, whilst securing it with one twist of wire with the other. One twist will be quite enough, and the next flower or leaf will hide the previous twist of wire. You will quickly see how close to place the next one.

5. Work along until you reach the top of the swag with your wire/sticky-tape marker, then go back and cover the other half of the swag.

6. Repeat with all the other swags, leaving enough space when you reach the markers to allow room to tie the ribbon bows.

7. Fix the swags to the tablecloth with large safety pins through the back of the bows. If your tablecloth is delicate, make sure you have an undercloth of something stouter to bear the weight.

8. Spray the swags with water just before you attach them to the table and they will last for several hours, but do choose your flowers carefully and avoid anything that will wilt quickly.

Puff Pastry

225 g/8 oz. plain flour
2.5 ml/½ tsp. salt
225 g/8 oz. cold unsalted butter
120 ml/4 fl. oz. cold water

Before you begin:

1. All the ingredients should be cold. Keep the flour in the refrigerator.

2. Work in as cool an area as possible, on a cold surface. Marble is ideal.

3. Puff pastry has six 'turns'. After the first turn, repeat the process so that a pair of turns has been made. Cover in plastic wrap and chill for 20 minutes. Then make a second pair of turns. If you intend to keep the dough in the refrigerator for a couple of days or freeze it before use, do so after 4 turns. If frozen, thaw in the refrigerator when required. Complete the final 2 turns and allow to rest once more in the refrigerator before rolling out for baking.

4. To remind you of how many turns have been made, at the end of each pair make 2 (or 4) light indentations in the dough with your fingertips.

5. Never allow the egg glaze to dribble down the sides of the rolled dough as this will seal the edges and stop the layers from rising properly.

1. Place the chilled flour and salt in a mixing bowl. Rub in 30 g/1 oz. of the butter, then add the water and quickly work with the fingers into a dough. Do not overhandle the dough. Alternatively, this stage can be done in a food processor. Wrap in clingfilm and chill for 10 minutes.

2. Lightly flour the remaining cold butter and place between two sheets of greaseproof paper. With a rolling pin, gently flatten into an 11-cm/4½-inch square. Chill for 10 minutes.

3. On a floured surface, roll out the dough to a 23-cm/9-inch square.

4. Remove the paper from the butter and place the butter diagonally across the centre of the dough.

5. Fold the dough in over the butter square so that it overlaps slightly in the middle like an envelope.

6. Press slightly with a rolling pin or the fingers to seal the edges and enclose the butter.

7. Make the first turn: place the pastry parcel seam-side down on a floured work surface. Roll out quickly and smoothly into a rectangle which is 2½ times as long as it is wide. Turn the pastry over and, holding the narrow end, fold in thirds.

8. Press down gently with the rolling pin to seal the 3 layers. This completes one turn.

Berry Charlotte

Serves 6

100 g/3½ oz. sugar
120 ml/4 fl. oz. water
45 ml/3 tbsp. fruit liqueur, such as framboise
1½ packets sponge fingers or ladyfingers (enough to line the inside of the mould)
480 ml/16 fl. oz. milk
5 ml/1 tsp. vanilla essence
5 egg yolks
200 g/7 oz. caster sugar
225 g/8 oz. puréed berries (raspberries, strawberries, blackberries)
1 sachet powdered gelatine
600 ml/1 pint double cream
450 g/1 lb. mixed fresh berries for garnish

1. Butter a 1.7-litre/3-pint soufflé dish or charlotte mould. In a small saucepan, dissolve the sugar in the water and bring to the boil. Remove from the heat and add the liqueur. Lay the ladyfingers flat side up on a tray and brush them with the syrup. Line the sides of the buttered mould with the ladyfingers, rounded side out and soaked side in. (The butter will help them stick to the mould.)

2. Bring the milk to the boil in a saucepan. While it is heating, whisk the egg yolks with the sugar and vanilla until light and pale. When the milk has come to the boil, pour it in a thin steady stream into the egg yolk mixture, whisking constantly. Put this mixture in the top of a double boiler and cook over simmering water, stirring constantly, until it has thickened and coats the back of a spoon. Add the gelatine to the hot custard according to the instructions on the packet. Stir in the berry purée and chill the mixture until it begins to thicken.

3. Whip half of the cream until it forms soft peaks. Stir ¼ of the cream into the thickened berry mixture and then carefully fold in the rest. Pour into the mould lined with ladyfingers and chill until set, at least 3 hours.

4. When the charlotte is set, carefully unmould it on to a serving plate. Whip the remaining cream until stiff, pipe a decorative border around the base and top of the charlotte and decorate with berries.

To make an 'ice bucket' you will need two watertight containers of suitable size – one slightly smaller than the other. I used two waste paper bins.

1. Pour about 4 cm/1½ inches of ordinary tap water into the larger container and freeze.

2. Now place the smaller container in the middle of the frozen 'base'. Fill it with easily removable heavy objects, to weight it down and prevent it from floating, and further secure it with a mesh of sticky-tape strips across the top of the larger container.

3. Now just poke whatever flowers and leaves you fancy down the space between the two containers. Don't pack them too tightly as you will destroy the lovely transparent effect as the light shines through the ice between the flowers. Fill up the space with water to just below the top of the inner container.

4. Freeze for at least 24 hours. Remove the sticky tape and weights and fill the inner container with very hot water. You will soon be able to lift it out easily. Dip the larger container in a sink of hot water and simply tip your 'ice bucket' out on to a tea towel (this catches any surplus water and guards against chipping).

1 metal or plastic waste paper bin
water ← freeze

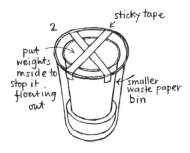

2 sticky tape
put weights inside to stop it floating out
smaller waste paper bin

3 fill space with water and freeze
push flowers and leaves in space

4 fill inner container with hot water and remove
dip in hot water and remove outer container

5. Replace in the freezer until required. You will find it easier to carry and handle wearing oven gloves. The same principle can be used to make lovely ice bowls for fruit salad, which can be replaced in the freezer once you have served out and re-used several times.

Berry Charlotte (see page 67) is here given the full romantic setting. A cheap grey metal plant stand, found minus its container in a junk shop, was painted pink, to act as a stand for an ordinary dinner plate, then decorated with fresh flowers. The spectacular ice bucket is made from real ice in which fresh flowers and leaves are suspended. Although it takes a good 24 hours to freeze, it takes only a few minutes to make.

Scorched Pepper and Beetroot Terrine (*see page 72*). A very effective table setting has been created here for very little cost. The knife, fork and spoons were found in a discount hardware shop for next to nothing as was the glass (three for the price of a glass of beer in a pub). The simplicity of the glass and cutlery, together with the classic design of the china, bought incredibly cheaply from a market stall, gives a very classy look and the little pattern on the cloth (a cheap remnant of dress fabric) picks up the design on the edge of the plates and exactly matches in colour. The garden flowers in the two old jugs soften the effect and give the table a personal touch.

Easy-to-prepare Buffet

Scorched Pepper and Beetroot Terrine
Five-spice Braised Beef
Curried Seafood Ring
Peanut, Cucumber and Onion Pilaf
Orange, Onion and Radicchio Salad
Bittersweet Chocolate Cream Pie
Apricot Pavlova

THIS easy-to-prepare menu costs surprisingly little to produce, yet will yield a lavish-looking and delicious spread for any party. All the recipes are served cold and, except for the puddings and dressing the salad, can all be prepared the day before. The quantities multiply easily to feed a crowd and the menu would be perfect for a teenage party or birthday. The terrine should be sliced and arranged on plates, ready for the guests and definitely served as a separate first course, whereas the rest of the food can be attractively displayed on a buffet table for everyone to help themselves.

Scorched Pepper and Beetroot Terrine

Serves 12

5 ml/1 tsp. caraway seeds
30 ml/2 tbsp. lemon juice
115 g/4 oz. cooked beetroot, peeled and chopped into tiny dice
salt and freshly ground black pepper
5 large red peppers, cored, seeded and cut into 4-cm/1½-inch strips
2 cloves garlic, peeled and crushed
2 sachets powdered gelatine
600 ml/1 pint double cream

1. Toast the caraway seeds in a dry frying pan over high heat for about 1 minute or until they begin to jump. Mix the seeds with the lemon juice, diced beetroot and salt and pepper to taste. Leave to marinate for 30 minutes.

2. Place the pepper strips in batches on kitchen foil under a hot grill, skin side up, and leave until skin is completely blackened, about 10–15 minutes. Place in a plastic bag and leave for 5 minutes. Remove the skins under a running tap, then dry the pepper strips on kitchen paper. Purée them with the garlic in a food processor or liquidiser, then push through a sieve. Dissolve the gelatine in 60 ml/4 tbsp. water according to the instructions on the packet and add to the purée. Mix well. Season generously with salt and pepper (mixture should be highly seasoned at this point, because the added cream will dilute the flavours). Whip the cream until it forms soft peaks. Fold in ¼ to slacken the pepper mixture, then fold in the rest thoroughly.

3. Oil 2 × 0.5 kg/1 lb. loaf tins. Pour ¼ of the mixture into each tin. Rap the tins sharply on the work surface to level the layer and eliminate any air bubbles. Place in the refrigerator for about 15 minutes or until just beginning to set, or in the freezer for about 5 minutes. Drain any excess liquid from the beetroot mixture and spread in an even layer in each tin. Pour over the remaining pepper mixture and rap again on the work surface. Chill in the refrigerator until set for at least 4 hours and up to 24 hours.

4. To unmould, dip the tins in hot water to loosen the terrines and turn out onto a platter or board. To serve, slice each terrine into 6 even slices with a hot, wet knife and place in the centre of chilled plates accompanied by melba toast or brown bread and butter.

Five-spice Braised Beef

Serves 12

30 ml/2 tbsp. vegetable oil
1.1 kg/2½ lb. rolled brisket of beef
3 cloves garlic, peeled and crushed
5 ml/1 tsp. salt
5 ml/1 tsp. freshly ground black pepper
7.5 ml/1½ tsp. five-spice powder
140 ml/¼ pint ginger wine
2 quantities vinaigrette dressing (see p. 42), made with 30 ml/2 tbsp. soy sauce in addition to the listed ingredients
1 large bunch spring onions, washed, trimmed and cut into thin strips

1. Heat oven to 220°C/gas mark 7. In a large frying pan or wok, heat the oil and brown the meat thoroughly all over. Transfer to a covered casserole and sprinkle with the garlic, salt, pepper and five-spice powder. Pour over the ginger wine, cover and cook in the preheated oven for 20 minutes. Reduce the heat to 140°C/gas mark 1 and continue cooking for 2 further hours, basting occasionally.

2. Remove the meat from the cooking juices, cover and let cool. With a sharp knife, cut the meat into 5-cm/¼-inch batons. Toss in a bowl with the vinaigrette until coated, then turn out on to an attractive plate or serving dish and garnish with the spring onion strips.

Curried Seafood Ring

Serves 12

225 g/8 oz. fresh spinach leaves, cleaned, with any thick stems discarded
450 g/1 lb. raw white fish fillets, skin and bones removed, cut into cubes
4 eggs
170 g/6 oz. wholemeal breadcrumbs
15 ml/1 tbsp. curry powder
85 g/3 oz. butter, melted
salt and freshly ground black pepper
2 hard-boiled eggs, roughly chopped
115 g/4 oz. cooked, shelled prawns, roughly chopped

1. Heat the oven to 180°C/gas mark 4. Blanch the spinach leaves by cooking them in boiling salted water for 1–2 minutes or until quite tender. Remove them from the water with a slotted spoon and plunge into a bowl of ice water – this will set the bright colour. Carefully lay the leaves out to dry on a clean tea towel or kitchen paper. Oil a 1.5-litre/2-pint ring mould.

2. In a food processor or liquidiser, purée the raw fish. Add the eggs, breadcrumbs, curry powder, melted butter and salt and pepper to taste and continue to process until the mixture is smooth.

3. Put the fish mixture in a bowl and stir in the chopped eggs and prawns.

4. Line the ring mould with the dried spinach leaves, draping the leaves over the edge. Fill the mould with the fish mixture using a spoon or small spatula. Smooth the top and fold over the leaves. Cover any gaps with more leaves, then cover the mould with kitchen foil. Put the mould in a bain-marie and cook in the preheated oven for 50–60 minutes, or until firm.

5. Leave to cool in the mould, then turn out and cut into 1-cm/½-inch slices.

Peanut, Cucumber and Onion Pilaf

Serves 12

60 ml/4 tbsp. vegetable oil
2 large onions, peeled and chopped
675 g/1½ lb. long-grain rice, preferably basmati, thoroughly washed under running water, then dried on a tea towel
2.3 litres/4 pints chicken stock, or enough to cover the rice in a saucepan by 2.5 cm/1 inch
115 g/4 oz. roasted, skinned peanuts, roughly chopped
½ cucumber, washed and cut into fine dice
30 ml/2 tbsp. finely chopped fresh parsley
salt and freshly ground black pepper

1. Heat the oil in a large lidded saucepan and cook the onion over a moderate heat, stirring occasionally, for about 5 minutes, or until soft and transparent. Add the rice and continue to cook, stirring constantly for 5 minutes. Pour over enough stock to cover the contents of the pan by 2.5 cm/1 inch.

2. Increase the heat and cook the rice over full heat, leaving the pan undisturbed. When all the stock has boiled away and the surface of the rice is pitted with little holes (about 10 minutes), remove from the heat, place a tea towel or two layers of kitchen paper over the top of the pan, then cover it with the lid. Leave for 30 minutes, during which the rice will continue to cook.

3. Fluff the rice with a fork, fold in the chopped peanuts, cucumber and parsley and season with salt and pepper to taste. Chill thoroughly before serving.

Orange, Onion and Radicchio Salad

Serves 12

6 oranges, peel and pith cut off
3 heads radicchio, washed and leaves separated
3 mild onions, peeled and sliced into thin rings
2 quantities vinaigrette dressing, (see p. 42), made with the reserved orange juice instead of lemon juice

1. Slice the oranges into thin rounds, working over a bowl to catch the juices. Use any reserved juice to make the vinaigrette, making up the required quantity with lemon juice or red wine vinegar. Toss the oranges, radicchio and onion with the vinaigrette and arrange attractively in a serving bowl.

Bittersweet Chocolate Cream Pie

Serves 12

1 quantity shortcrust pastry (see p. 43)
1 egg, separated
240 ml/8 fl. oz. milk
200 g/7 oz. best quality plain chocolate, broken into small pieces
3 eggs
60 g/2 oz. caster sugar
140 ml/¼ pint double cream
icing sugar for decoration

1. Heat the oven to 190°C/gas mark 5. Roll out the pastry thinly and line a 25-cm/10-inch loose bottomed flan tin. (You will have pastry left over—freeze it for another use). Prick the bottom of the crust with a fork and bake the crust blind for 15 minutes. Remove the tin from the oven and paint the inside of the hot pastry with the egg white to form a glaze that will prevent the filling from making the pastry soggy.

2. In a small saucepan, combine the milk and the chocolate and cook over very low heat for about 10 minutes, stirring occasionally, until all the chocolate is melted and blended. Be careful not to scorch the chocolate.

3. In a mixing bowl, whisk together the eggs, egg yolk, sugar and cream. Let the chocolate mixture cool slightly and whisk it into the egg mixture. Carefully pour the filling into the crust and return it to the oven. Reduce the heat to 160°C/gas mark 3 and bake for a further 45 minutes or until the custard is just set (the centre will still feel slightly wobbly). Let the tart cool, then remove the flan tin. Dust the top of the tart with icing sugar.

Apricot Pavlova

Serves 12

6 egg whites
300 g/10½ oz. caster sugar
pinch of salt
7.5 ml/1½ tsp. white vinegar

Filling:

340 g/12 oz. dried apricots, soaked in water to cover for 4 hours, then drained
juice of 3 oranges
grated zest of 1½ oranges
450 ml/¾ pint double cream

1. Heat the oven to 150°C/gas mark 2. Cut 4 × 23-cm/9-inch circles from greaseproof paper. Place a circle in each of two 23-cm/9-inch cake tins, wet one side of the remaining two circles and place them, wet side down, on the first circles. (The water sandwiched between the paper will make the bottom of the meringues crisp and easy to remove from the paper.)

2. Beat the egg whites with half the sugar, the salt and the vinegar until very stiff. Add the rest of the sugar carefully and beat to form a glossy meringue.

3. Spread the meringue on the paper circles to within 2.5 cm/1 inch of the border. Bake for 30 minutes in the preheated oven, then reduce the heat to 140°C gas/mark 1 and continue baking for 30 minutes. Remove the meringues from the tins, carefully peel off the paper, and allow to cool on a rack.

4. For the filling: in a small saucepan cook the apricots, orange rind and juice over a medium heat until very soft, about 45 minutes. Purée the mixture. Stiffly whip the cream and carefully fold into the apricot purée.

5. Put one meringue circle on a serving dish, spread with half the apricot cream, place the other meringue circle on the cream and spread the remaining apricot cream over the top.

Opposite: Apricot Pavlova. This sinful and delicious Australian invention is prettily decorated with borage flowers, which contrast perfectly with the apricot cream whilst echoing the deep blue border of the cake stand. Fresh flowers can make the most effective garnishes for both sweet and savoury dishes, but do check that they are edible first.

Sit-down Seafood Supper

Manhattan Seafood Chowder
Bacon-wrapped Trout Fillets
Potatoes Dauphinois
Muscadet-marinated Fruit Salad

THIS IS A delicious fishy meal which is ideal for a small lunch or dinner party. Alternatively, provided you have the kitchen facilities, these recipes can simply be multiplied to feed as many as you want.

When feeding a lot of people, it is important to choose a menu that everyone will like, to avoid the extra work of offering alternatives. Fish, therefore, is often an excellent choice and forms the basis of the first two courses of this meal.

Manhattan Seafood Chowder

Serves 6

2 large potatoes, peeled and diced
30 ml/2 tbsp. olive oil
1 onion, peeled and chopped
4 stalks celery, washed and chopped
2 × 395 g/14 oz. tins peeled Italian tomatoes, with reserved liquid
2 cloves garlic, peeled and crushed
30 ml/2 tbsp. chopped fresh parsley
1.1 litres/2 pints fish or chicken stock
225 g/8 oz. white fish fillet, skin and bones removed, cut into 2.5-cm/1-inch cubes
170 g/6 oz. cockles, shelled and rinsed (not the kind sold in vinegar)
15 g/4 oz. cooked prawns, shelled
salt and freshly ground black pepper

1. In a medium-sized saucepan, parboil the potatoes by cooking them in boiling salted water for 10 minutes, until partly tender. Drain.

2. In a large pan, heat the olive oil and cook the onion and celery until soft but not brown, about 10 minutes. Add the tomatoes and their liquid, garlic, parsley, stock and parboiled potatoes and simmer 30 minutes, until all the vegetables are tender.

3. Bring mixture to a boil and add the cubes of fish. Boil gently for 5 minutes, then add the cockles and prawns and simmer for 5 further minutes until the fish is no longer translucent in the middle and the cockles and prawns are heated through. Season well with salt and pepper and pour into warmed soup bowls to serve.

Bacon-wrapped Trout Fillets

Serves 6

6 × 115 g/4 oz. trout fillets, skin and small bones removed
salt and freshly gound black pepper
15 ml/1 tbsp. fresh thyme or 7.5 ml/1½ tsp. dried
juice of ½ lemon
170–225 g/6–8 oz. (24 rashers) very thin smoked streaky rindless bacon

1. Heat the grill. Sprinkle the trout with salt, pepper, thyme and lemon juice. Fold each fillet in half lengthwise, then cut in half. Wrap each piece with 2 rashers of bacon and secure with toothpicks if necessary. Lay the trout on a lightly-oiled grill pan and grill 5 minutes on each side until the bacon is slightly crispy and the fish is cooked. Remove the toothpicks, if used, and serve 2 pieces of trout per person.

Potatoes Dauphinois

Serves 6

1.4 kg/3 lb. potatoes, peeled and cut into very thin slices (see note)
300 ml/½ pint milk
115 g/4 oz. butter
170 g/6 oz. grated gruyère cheese
1 clove garlic, peeled and crushed
salt and freshly ground black pepper
freshly grated nutmeg

1. Put the potatoes and milk in a large saucepan and boil about 10 minutes or until they are partly tender, taking care not to burn the milk.

2. Heat the oven to 180°C/gas mark 4. With 30 g/1 oz. of the butter, grease a shallow ovenproof dish. Using a slotted spoon, remove the potatoes from the milk and layer them in the dish with the grated cheese and crushed garlic, dotting with remaining butter and seasoning with salt, pepper and nutmeg. Pour the milk over the potatoes and sprinkle with a bit more cheese. Bake in the preheated oven approximately 1½ hours or until the potatoes are very tender.

NOTE: Do not wash the potatoes once they are peeled and sliced as this would remove the starch that gives this dish its creamy homogeneous texture.

Muscadet-marinated Fruit Salad

Serves 6

1.7 litres/3 pints fresh fruit, washed, peeled and cut into 1-cm/½-inch cubes (see note)
45 ml/3 tbsp. caster sugar
180 ml/6 fl. oz. muscadet or other crisp white wine
180 ml/6 fl. oz. double cream, whipped, and mint leaves for garnish

1. Put all the prepared fruit into a large bowl, sprinkle with the sugar and pour over the wine. Leave to marinate in the refrigerator at least 2 hours and up to 12 hours, tossing occasionally.

2. Divide the fruit salad between 6 individual plates and garnish with the whipped cream and mint leaves.

NOTE: I have not given weights for the fruit, as this obviously would vary with the types of fruit you choose. Buy a selection that is varied in colour, texture and flavour. I never find bananas very successful in a fruit salad, as they quickly go rather slimy.

Slimline Gourmet Fare

**Filo Pastry Purses with Salmon
and Spring Onions
Chicken and Asparagus Poached in Herb
Tea with Nettle Sauce
Banana Yogurt Ice Cream with
Blackcurrant Sauce**

NOBODY WANTS to cook two separate menus at the same meal, yet those who are seriously trying to slim often find it difficult to produce a really delicious meal for guests that will be permitted on their own strictly controlled diet. Doesn't really special food rely on cooking with lots of wine, butter, cream and sugar? This menu proves that it doesn't.

Designed to suit the poshest of occasions, although quite within the regime of the strictest weight watcher, it not only looks stunning, but tastes spectacular and will satisfy even those with the heartiest appetites. If you are nervous that your guests might leave the table hungry, make a hot, creamy soup from fresh vegetables, simply puréed in the stock in which they were cooked and serve it at the beginning of the meal.

Opposite: Chicken and Asparagus Poached in Herb Tea with Nettle Sauce (*see page 85*).

Filo Pastry Purses with Salmon and Spring Onions

Serves 6

1 egg, beaten
60 ml/4 tbsp. fromage frais (the 'virtually fat free' variety)
250 g/9 oz. cooked salmon, bones removed, flaked
45 ml/3 tbsp. sliced spring onions
15 ml/1 tbsp. lemon juice
salt and white pepper
6 sheets filo pastry
45 ml/3 tbsp. oil, for brushing

Sauce:

270 ml/9 fl. oz. plain low-fat yogurt
45 ml/3 tbsp. lemon juice
salt and white pepper
30 ml/2 tbsp. sliced spring onions
¼ cucumber, very thinly sliced

1. Heat the oven to 200°C/gas mark 6. In a bowl, combine the egg and fromage frais and mix well. Add the salmon, spring onions, lemon juice and salt and pepper to taste.
2. Lay out one sheet of filo pastry with the long sides vertical. Brush the lower half of the sheet with oil, fold over the top half and brush with oil, then trim sides to form a 17.5-cm/7-inch square. Place 1/6 of the filling in the centre of the square and gather up all the edges of the pastry to form a little purse, pinching to seal.
3. Place the purses on a greased baking tray and bake in the preheated oven for 20–30 minutes until evenly golden-brown.
4. To make the sauce, combine all ingredients and taste for seasoning.

5. To serve, divide the cucumber slices between 6 plates and arrange to form a circle around the edge of each plate. Spoon a little sauce in the centre and set the filo purses on top.

NOTE: A little oil is necessary in this recipe to make the filo leaves stay separated and crisp, but this works out to only a little over 5 ml/1 tsp. per person and there is no other fat anywhere in the meal.

Chicken and Asparagus Poached in Herb Tea with Nettle Sauce

Serves 6

6 cloves garlic, skins left on
6 large spears asparagus, trimmed and woody ends discarded
6 boneless, skinless chicken breasts
salt and freshly ground black pepper
3–4 sprigs fresh parsley, washed and dried
3–4 leaves fresh sorrel, washed and dried
2 sprigs fresh thyme, washed and dried
3–4 sprigs fresh tarragon, washed and dried
2 spring onions, washed and trimmed
1 pot lemon verbena tea, or other herbal tea, cooled
170 g/6 oz. young nettle leaves (see note)
lemon juice
1 punnet cherry tomatoes, hulled and halved
steamed rice to serve

1. Put the garlic cloves in a pan of cold water and bring to the boil. Drain the water and repeat the process two more times. Remove the skins and reserve garlic.

2. Cook the asparagus in boiling salted water for 10 minutes, or until just tender. 'Butterfly' the chicken breasts by cutting them almost in half horizontally and opening them out like a book. Pound lightly to flatten between 2 sheets of cling film. Sprinkle with salt and pepper to taste, lay an asparagus spear in the centre, roll up and secure with toothpicks. In a sauté pan large enough to hold all the chicken breasts snugly in one layer, put the fresh herbs and spring onions in a layer on the bottom. Lay the chicken breasts on top, then pour in the cold tea until it just covers the chicken. Bring to a gentle boil and poach for 5 minutes. Remove the breasts, discard the cocktail sticks, cover the breasts and keep warm. Strain the poaching liquid and reserve; discard the solids.

3. Cook the nettles in lightly salted water for about 5 minutes or until completely wilted; drain. Put the cooked nettles, garlic, lemon juice and salt and pepper to taste in a food processor or liquidiser and purée. Add 120–150 ml/4–5 fl. oz. poaching liquid to the puréed nettles to finish the sauce.

4. Put the tomato halves on a lightly oiled baking tray, sprinkle with salt and pepper and grill for 3–5 minutes until hot and bubbling.

5. To serve, slice the chicken into 1-cm/½-inch rounds. Divide the sauce between 6 heated dinner plates and lay the chicken slices in an arc on top. Pile the grilled tomatoes on the plates and serve with steamed rice.

NOTE: The herbs suggested are merely a guideline; use whatever fresh herbs you can find.

NOTE: If you have never cooked with stinging nettles, try it; you will be pleasantly surprised. Ideally, the new shoots in early spring are the best, otherwise take only the very small leaves from the top of each plant. Gloves must obviously be worn to protect your hands from nasty stings when picking, and don't gather nettles that grow too close to a road that carries a lot of traffic. If no nettles are available, you can substitute fresh spinach.

Banana Yogurt Ice Cream with Blackcurrant Sauce

Makes About 570 ml/1 pint

4 very ripe bananas

300 ml/½ pint low-fat yogurt

freshly grated nutmeg

Sauce:

210 g/7½ oz. tin blackcurrants in
natural fruit juice

1. Put the bananas, yogurt and a pinch of nutmeg in a liquidiser or food processor and process until smooth. Pour the mixture into a container and freeze for 1–2 hours until firm. The texture of the yogurt is best when made within 6 hours of serving. If it freezes very hard, put it in the refrigerator 2 hours before serving to soften.

2. For the sauce, purée blackcurrants and juice in a liquidiser or food processor. For a completely smooth texture, push through a fine sieve.

Hot and Hearty Summer Supper

**Warm Salmon and Vegetable
Terrine with Salad Greens
Honey-roasted Poussins
Artichoke Pilaf
Apricot Pancakes with
Honey–Orange Sauce**

THIS TASTY MENU, although ideal for an intimate gathering, could be expanded perfectly to suit any large number of people gathering for a hot sit-down meal. The recipes, although far from heavy, are designed to be substantial enough to satisfy guests who have, perhaps, spent a sporty day outdoors.

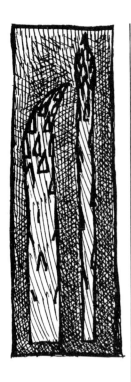

Warm Salmon and Vegetable Terrine with Salad Greens

Serves 6

115 g/4 oz. asparagus spears, ends trimmed
1 large carrot, peeled and cut into long batons
450 g/1 lb. salmon fillets, skin and bones removed, cut into large dice
2.5 ml/½ tsp. salt
2 egg whites
freshly ground black pepper
freshly grated nutmeg
10 ml/2 tsp. lemon juice
grated zest of 1 lemon
300 ml/½ pint double cream
170 g/6 oz. mixed salad greens
1 quantity vinaigrette dressing (see p. 42)

1 quantity vinaigrette dressing (see p. 42)

1. Cook the asparagus and carrot in boiling water for about 15 minutes until very tender. Drain and dry thoroughly on a tea towel. Trim to fit the length of a 1-kg/2-lb. loaf tin. (If they are not long enough, piece two together.) Set the vegetables aside.

2. In a food processor, purée the fish with the salt, then add the egg whites and season with pepper, nutmeg, lemon juice and zest. Transfer the mixture to a bowl and chill in the refrigerator for 30 minutes. Remove from the refrigerator and using a wooden spoon, beat in the cream. Do not overbeat at this point or the cream may separate.

3. Heat the oven to 180°C/gas mark 4. Oil a 1-kg/2-lb. loaf tin. Spread half of the salmon mixture on the bottom of the tin. Rap it sharply on the work surface to eliminate any bubbles. Arrange the asparagus and carrot strips lengthways in a layer on top. Spread the remaining salmon on top of the vegetables. Rap again on the work surface. Cover the tin with kitchen foil. Cook in a bain-marie in the preheated oven for 50–60 minutes. Remove from the oven and leave to cool in the bain-marie for 10 minutes, then unmould and slice into 6 even slices.

4. Lay the slices on individual plates. Toss the salad leaves in vinaigrette and arrange around the terrine, which is best served warm.

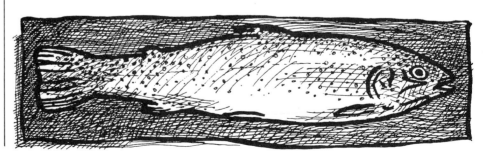

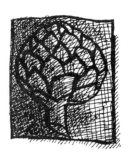

Honey-roasted Poussins

Serves 6

3 large poussins, approximately 450 g/1 lb. each
salt and freshly ground black pepper
1 carrot, washed and roughly chopped
1 leek, washed and roughly chopped
1 onion, skin left on, roughly chopped
1 bunch parsley
1 bay leaf
10 ml/2 tsp. fresh thyme or 5 ml/1 tsp. dried

Glaze:

30 ml/2 tbsp. honey
30 ml/2 tbsp. soy sauce
30 ml/2 tbsp. water

 1 desertspoon of each is enough.

1. Heat the oven to 220°C/gas mark 7. Sprinkle the poussins with salt and pepper and place them in a large roasting tin with the carrot, leek, onion, parsley, bay leaf and thyme. Add enough water to come about halfway up the poussins (1.1–1.7 litres/2–3 pints), then cover the tin tightly with kitchen foil and bake in the preheated oven for 45–50 minutes, until the poussins are just tender and the juices run clear when pricked with a knife. Remove the poussins from the tin. Sieve the cooking liquid, discarding solids, and reserve.

2. Fifteen minutes before serving, heat the oven to 250°C/gas mark 9. Cut each poussin in half lengthways and lay it cutside down on a kitchen foil-covered baking tray. Mix together the honey, soy sauce and water and brush the poussins thoroughly with this glaze. Season with salt and pepper. Place the poussins in the hot oven and roast for 10–15 minutes, until the skins are brown and crispy. Serve hot.

NOTE: Poussins are small chickens, available from many large supermarkets.

Artichoke Pilaf

Serves 6

30 ml/2 tbsp. olive oil
1 medium-sized onion, peeled and chopped
340 g/12 oz. long-grain rice, preferably basmati, thoroughly rinsed under cool water and dried on a tea towel
60 g/2 oz. mixed dried fruit
1.1 litres/2 pints light chicken or vegetable stock
1 × 395 g/14 oz. tin artichoke hearts, drained and quartered
salt and freshly ground black pepper

1. In a heavy-bottomed lidded saucepan, heat the oil and cook the onion over a moderate heat, stirring frequently, for 5 minutes until soft and transparent. Add the rice and stir to coat all the grains with the oil. Stir in the mixed fruit and pour over the stock to cover the contents of the pan by 2.5 cm/1 inch. Increase the heat and cook the rice over full heat, leaving the pan undisturbed. When all the stock has boiled away and the surface of the rice is pitted with little holes (about 10 minutes), remove from the heat. Put the artichoke quarters on the rice and lay a tea towel or two layers of kitchen paper over the top of the pan, then cover with the lid. Leave for 30 minutes, during which the rice will continue to cook, absorbing its own steam and the artichokes will be heated through.

2. Just before serving, fluff the pilaf with a fork and season to taste with salt and pepper.

Apricot Pancakes with Honey–orange Sauce

Serves 6

115 g/4 oz. plain flour
2 eggs
1.25 ml/¼ tsp. salt
420 ml/14 fl. oz. milk
oil for frying

Filling:

340 g/12 oz. dried apricots
5 ml/1 tsp. ground ginger
85 g/3 oz. butter

Sauce:

75 ml/5 tbsp. honey
juice of 2 oranges

1. In a medium-sized bowl, mix together the flour, eggs, salt and milk to make a smooth batter. Allow to rest for 1 hour.

2. In a medium-sized frying pan, preferably non-stick, brush a thin coating of oil in the bottom of the pan and pour in a small amount of batter, turning the pan so the batter spreads to a thin layer. Cook until the pancakes begin to brown on the edges, then, using a fish slice or a spatula, flip the pancake and cook the other side. Continue until all the batter is used. You should have 12 pancakes.

3. To make the apricot filling, soak the apricots and ground ginger in 450 ml/¾ pint water for 4 hours. Put in a small saucepan and cook over a low heat, partially covered, until all the water has evaporated and the apricots are very soft. (Be careful not to burn the apricots.) Purée the mixture in a food processor or liquidiser.

4. To make the sauce, heat the honey and orange juice in a small saucepan and stir to combine.

5. To finish, spread 1 tbsp. filling on each pancake to within 2.5 cm/1 inch of the edge. Roll up the bottom third of the pancake, fold in 2.5 cm/1 inch on each side, then continue rolling up to make a shape like a Chinese spring roll. Pack into a buttered shallow ovenproof dish.

6. To serve, dot the top of the rolled pancakes with butter and heat in the oven at 190°C/gas mark 5 for 20 minutes or until heated through. Put two pancakes on each plate and pour over a little sauce.

Cook-ahead Cuisine

Avocado Salad with Walnuts and
Caper–Lemon Dressing
Mediterranean Lamb with Olives
(or Grapes)
Easy-cook Pasta
Honey–Whisky Ice Cream with
Marmalade Sauce

FOR THOSE who lead very busy lives and like to provide something a little out of the ordinary for their guests, here is an imaginative menu with a definite Mediterranean touch in the first two courses, rounded off with a delicious ice cream with an unusual Scottish twist.

Most of the preparation for the recipes can be completed earlier in the day, or the evening before, leaving the cook with very little last-minute preparation, free to enjoy the guests.

Some supermarkets now sell boned and rolled legs of lamb, which would be perfect for the main course, making the task of carving much easier. Potatoes in their jackets would make a good alternative to the pasta.

Mediterranean Lamb with Olives (*see page* 95).

Avocado Salad with Walnuts and Caper–Lemon Dressing

Serves 6

1 clove garlic, peeled and crushed
30 ml/2 tbsp. lemon juice
5 ml/1 tsp. Dijon mustard
120 ml/4 fl. oz. olive oil
15 ml/1 tbsp. capers, coarsely chopped
salt and freshly ground black pepper
3 ripe avocados, peeled, halved and stoned
85 g/3 oz. walnuts, chopped

1. Combine garlic, lemon juice, mustard, olive oil capers and salt and pepper to taste in a screw-topped jar and shake well to mix.
2. Place each avocado half cut-side down on a work surface and cut across into 0.5-cm/¼-inch slices. Carefully lift each half onto a plate and spread the slices into a fan. Drizzle the dressing over the avocado and garnish with the chopped walnuts.

Mediterranean Lamb with Olives (or Grapes)

Serves 6

45 ml/3 tbsp. olive oil
1.4–1.8 kg/3–4 lb. leg of lamb
2 medium-sized onions, peeled and chopped
225 g/8 oz. mushrooms, wiped and sliced
½ bottle red wine
300 ml/½ pint beef stock (see note)
3–4 cloves garlic, peeled and crushed
salt and freshly ground black pepper
15 ml/1 tbsp. fresh rosemary or 7.5 ml/1½ tsp. dried
18 large black olives, stoned (or 36 seedless grapes)
5-cm/2-inch strip of lemon zest
60 ml/4 tbsp. concentrated tomato purée

1. Heat the oven to 150°C/gas mark 2. Heat the oil in a heavy flameproof casserole and brown the lamb on all sides. Remove and set aside. Add the onions to the pan and cook for 3–4 minutes until transparent. Add the mushrooms and cook for 2–3 minutes stirring constantly. Add all the remaining ingredients to the pan and bring to the boil, stirring until all are well mixed. Alternatively, brown the meat and vegetables in a frying or sauté pan and transfer them to an ovenproof casserole. (If you are using grapes instead of olives, reserve half and add to the casserole for the last 15 minutes of the cooking.)
2. Return the lamb to the pan, turning and basting to make sure it is well coated with sauce. Cover the pan and cook in the preheated oven for 2½–3 hours. To serve, cut into thick slices, spoon over the sauce and serve with buttered pasta and fresh seasonable vegetables or a green salad.

NOTE: If using stock cubes, buy the kind which have no additives, or even better, use canned beef consommé for a richer, more luxurious flavour. If you do not have a large enough lidded casserole, use a deep baking tin or dish and make a domed 'lid' with kitchen foil.

You could cook this dish over a longer period in a *very* slow oven or slow cooker if it fits in better with your schedule – up to 8 hours. It can be cooked in advance, frozen, then thawed (allow plenty of time) and reheated on the day or it can simply be cooked the day before, kept in the fridge and reheated for almost 30 minutes in a moderate oven just before required.

NOTE: I have given an alternative recipe using grapes for those people who don't like olives. However, I have served the original version to people who *think* they don't like olives and they've loved it!

Easy-cook Pasta

Serves 6

360 g/12 oz. pasta shells, bows or other small shapes
60 g/2 oz. butter
freshly ground black pepper

1. Plunge the pasta into a large pan of salted boiling water. After it returns to the boil, simmer for 3 minutes. Turn off the heat and cover the pan tightly with a lid. Leave the pan undisturbed for the length of time the instructions on the packet say the pasta would take to cook normally. The pasta will now be perfectly cooked. Drain and toss with butter and pepper to taste.

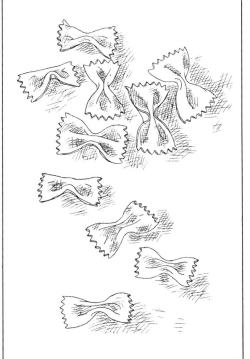

Honey–whisky Ice Cream with Marmalade Sauce

Makes 1.1 litres/2 pints

6 egg yolks
140 ml/¼ pint honey
45 ml/3 tbsp. whisky
300 ml/½ pint double cream

Marmalade Sauce:

45 ml/3 tbsp. bitter orange marmalade
45 ml/3 tbsp. whisky
45 ml/3 tbsp. water

1. In a large bowl, beat the egg yolks until very light and fluffy. In a small saucepan, heat the honey until just boiling.

2. Pour the hot honey in a thin steady stream over the egg yolks, beating constantly. Keep beating vigorously until the mixture is cool and the yolks have increased in volume. Add the whisky and stir well to combine.

3. Whip the cream to soft peaks. Carefully fold into the egg yolk mixture, blending well. Pour the ice cream into a bowl and freeze for at least 8 hours before serving.

4. To make the sauce, combine all the ingredients in a small saucepan and simmer over a low heat until the marmalade is melted. Leave to cool.

NOTE: This sinfully delicious ice cream has the added bonus that it is soft enough to be easily spooned out straight from the freezer.

Formal Vegetarian Dinner

Chestnut Pâté Tartlets
Tagliatelle with Asparagus Cream Sauce
Black Forest Soufflé Pie

MANY 'MEAT' people shudder at the thought of being invited to a vegetarian dinner, fearing an indigestible mixture of boring food in varying shades of brown and beige. Here is a menu for a really elegant lunch or dinner party which will appeal to even the most fastidious of vegetarians and non-vegetarians alike. It is light and delicious and, with a little extra care in presentation, will rival a meal in the most chic restaurant.

Opposite: Tagliatelle with Asparagus Cream Sauce (*see* page 101). If you prefer to buy plates with some colour or pattern rather than classic plain white, choose something with the colour or design as a border. A pattern in the centre will only be hidden by the food and an all-over design can simply look messy. Some busy designs or strong colours overpower the food, so choose something that will enhance your dish like this, where the soft green border complements the greens of the asparagus and herbs.

Chestnut Pâté Tartlets

Makes 6

1 medium-sized onion, peeled and finely chopped
15 ml/1 tbsp. olive oil
2 cloves garlic, peeled and crushed
85 g/3 oz. fresh wholemeal breadcrumbs
30 ml/2 tbsp. finely chopped parsley
30 ml/2 tbsp. finely chopped spring onion
1 stalk celery, finely chopped
1 small hard apple, peeled and very finely chopped
15 ml/1 tbsp. lemon juice
280 g/10 oz. unsweetened chestnut purée (I use 10 oz. whole chestnuts, whizzed)
grated rind and juice of 1 orange
salt and freshly ground black pepper
6 10-cm/4-inch cooked individual shortcrust tartlet cases
4 oz. mixed bitter salad greens, washed and leaves separated
1 quantity vinaigrette dressing (see p. 42)

(see p. 42)

1. In a small pan, cook the onion in the oil until transparent, add the garlic and leave to cool. Mix the breadcrumbs with the parsley, spring onion and celery. Mix the finely chopped apple with the lemon juice to prevent discolouring. Add to the breadcrumb mixture. With a fork, mash the chestnut purée with the orange rind and juice until smooth and soft. Add with the cooked onion to the rest of the ingredients and season with salt and pepper to taste. Chill the pâté for at least 2 hours for the flavours to develop, then spoon into the tartlet cases.

2. To serve, toss the salad greens in the vinaigrette. Divide the salad between 6 individual plates and place one tartlet in the centre of each plate.

NOTE: For the salad, use as wide a variety of leaves as possible, i.e., watercress, chicory, rocket, frisée, radicchio, etc. Excellent bags of ready-washed mixed salad leaves are available from many supermarkets.

Tagliatelle with Asparagus Cream Sauce

Serves 6

675 g/1½ lb. fresh asparagus, cleaned, with woody ends trimmed off
450 ml/¾ pint single cream
salt and freshly ground black pepper
675 g/1½ lb. vacuum-packed or fresh white tagliatelle
fresh flat-leaved parsley, dill and snipped chives to garnish

1. Cut off the asparagus tips and set aside. Boil the asparagus stalks in salted water for about 15 minutes or until very tender. Remove the stalks with a slotted spoon and leave the water in the pan to cook the asparagus tips. In a food processor or liquidiser, purée the stalks with the cream and return to a clean pan. Reheat and season to taste with salt and pepper.
2. Boil the asparagus tips for 5 minutes in the reserved water until just tender.
3. Cook the pasta in boiling salted water for 3 minutes or until 'al dente'. Drain well.
4. Pour the sauce in a circle around the edge of individual serving plates. Pile the cooked pasta in the centre of the circles of sauce and arrange the cooked asparagus tips on top. Garnish with the fresh herbs and serve immediately.

NOTE: If no other fresh herbs are available, use just parsley.

Black Forest Soufflé Pie

Serves 6

2 × 280 g/10 oz. tins dark cherries, drained and stoned
30–45 ml/2–3 tbsp. cherry liqueur or brandy
4 eggs, separated
60 g/2 oz. caster sugar
60 g/2 oz. cocoa powder
icing sugar for dusting
240 ml/8 fl. oz. double cream, whipped

1. Heat the oven to 200°C/gas mark 6. Generously butter a 1.7-litre/3-pint soufflé dish and pour in the drained cherries. Sprinkle with liqueur and set aside.
2. Beat the egg yolks for 5 minutes, until thick and light. Beat the egg whites until they form soft peaks, then beat in the sugar, one tablespoonful at a time to form a glossy meringue. Carefully beat in the cocoa powder 1 tablespoonful at a time and beat until the mixture is stiff, but not dry. Put ¼ of the egg white mixture into the egg yolks and stir to slacken the mixture, then carefully fold in the remaining egg whites.
3. Spoon the soufflé mixture over the cherries, smoothing the surface with a spatula. Bake in the preheated oven for 20–25 minutes, until puffed and brown. Remove from the oven and dust with icing sugar. Serve warm with the whipped cream.

High-speed Cuisine

Warm Avocado, Feta and Bacon Salad
Seafood-stuffed Croissants
Sweet Chestnut Purée with Fromage Frais

 A PERFECT MENU for anyone who wants to produce an out-of-the-ordinary dinner in the shortest time possible – ideal for last-minute guests or simply for mid-week entertaining when both time and energy are running very short, but where something rather special to eat is called for.

Opposite: Warm Avocado, Feta and Bacon Salad (*see over*) in a charming simple setting. The blue of the jug and plates and the yellow of the seersucker cloth match the colours in the striped curtains of my kitchen to create a fresh, sunny look. The eye-catching flowers are no more than a few sprigs of gypsophila, salvaged from an old, discarded arrangement and padded out with some ordinary dandelion clocks.

Warm Avocado, Feta and Bacon Salad

Serves 6

170 g/6 oz. mixed salad leaves, washed, dried, leaves separated
2 ripe avocados
juice of 1 lemon
225 g/8 oz. smoked streaky bacon, cut into narrow strips diagonally
45 ml/3 tbsp. olive oil
2 cloves garlic, peeled and crushed
freshly ground black pepper
280 g/10 oz. feta cheese, cut into small cubes

1. Arrange the salad leaves on individual plates. Peel, halve and stone the avocados, slice them thinly and gently toss in 15 ml/1 tbsp. of the lemon juice.

2. Fry the bacon until crisp. Remove from the pan and keep warm. Add the olive oil and garlic to the pan with the remaining lemon juice. Season to taste with pepper and stir over a low heat until hot and well amalgamated.

3. Scatter the bacon, avocado and feta cheese over the salad leaves. Drizzle the hot dressing over and serve immediately.

NOTE: Mixed salad leaves are available washed and ready for use in plastic bags from many good supermarkets.

Seafood-stuffed Croissants

Serves 6

6 croissants
60 g/2 oz. butter
2 spring onions, trimmed and sliced, including the green part
115 g/4 oz. mushrooms, wiped and sliced
300 ml/½ pint double cream
2 cloves garlic, peeled and crushed
salt and freshly ground black pepper
170 g/6 oz. white fish fillets, skin and bones removed, cut into small cubes
170 g/6 oz. shelled prawns, thawed if frozen
170 g/6 oz. shelled cockles, rinsed
chopped dill or parsley to garnish

1. Heat the oven to 220°C/gas mark 7. Put the croissants in the oven to heat through.

2. Melt the butter in a medium-sized saucepan and cook the spring onions and mushrooms over a low heat, stirring occasionally, for 2–3 minutes. Add the cream and garlic and season to taste with salt and pepper. Allow to simmer gently for 1 minute, then add the fish and continue to cook for 1–2 minutes. Add the prawns and cockles and cook for one more minute.

3. To serve, split the croissants in half horizontally and place a base on each of 6 large plates. Spoon the fish and sauce over, allowing it to spill over onto the plate. Sprinkle with the chopped herbs and replace the croissant tops. Serve with plain steamed or boiled green vegetables.

NOTE: The sauce can be made in advance up to the point just before adding the fish. Reheat and add the fish when you bring out the plates from the first course. Don't be afraid to serve frozen vegetables at a formal dinner; some, like peas, broad beans and spinach, can be excellent if you are short of time.

Sweet Chestnut Purée with Fromage Frais

Serves 6

2 × 450 g/1 lb. cartons fromage frais

120 ml/6 heaped tbsp. sweetened chestnut purée

1. Divide the fromage frais between 6 small glasses or pretty bowls. Garnish with a spoonful of chestnut purée.

NOTE: Fromage frais or fromage blanc is a soft creamy white 'fresh' cheese and is available from many supermarkets. Some is virtually fat-free and excellent for slimmers, although the delicious sweetened chestnut purée used in this recipe is definitely not! Chestnut purée is available from large supermarkets, delicatessens and specialist food shops.

Medallions of Lamb with Roasted Garlic Sauce (*see over*). Food always looks good on white plates, but they don't necessarily have to be plain, and there are many different sorts of china for sale with a raised border pattern like this old Wedgwood plate.

Elegant 'Oven-ready' Dinner

Twice-cooked Cheese Soufflés
Medallions of Lamb with
Roasted Garlic Sauce
Sesame French Beans

 A MENU FOR a special dinner party which, with careful planning and a little advance preparation, requires next to no work at the last minute. A selection of fresh fruit, perhaps with some of the more exotic tropical fruits like lychees, mangoes, passion fruit, etc., now widely available, makes an effortless and perfect finish to this elegant meal, balancing the first two rather rich courses.

Twice-cooked Cheese Soufflés

Serves 6

85 g/3 oz. butter
85 g/3 oz. flour
450 ml/¾ pint milk
5 ml/1 tsp. mustard powder
salt and freshly ground black pepper
freshly grated nutmeg
340 g/12 oz. grated cheese (see note)
6 eggs, separated
450 ml/¾ pint double cream

1. Heat the oven to 190°C/gas mark 5. Melt the butter in a small saucepan, add the flour and cook for 3–4 minutes, stirring constantly with a wooden spoon. Add the milk, whisking constantly to avoid lumps, then add the mustard powder, salt, pepper and nutmeg. Bring to the boil and add half the grated cheese; stir to melt. The mixture will be very thick.
2. Pour the mixture into a bowl, let cool slightly, and stir in the egg yolks. Beat the egg whites until stiff, stir in ¼ of the egg whites into the cheese mixture to slacken it, then carefully fold in the rest of the whites. Pour into 6 buttered ramekins or ovenproof moulds and place in a bain-marie. Bake in the preheated oven for 30 minutes until risen and quite firm. Leave to cool.
3. Turn the cooled soufflés out into individual gratin dishes, or other small ovenproof shallow dishes, cover with the remaining grated cheese and pour over the cream. Heat the oven to 220°C/gas mark 7 and cook the soufflés for 20–25 minutes, until cheese and cream are bubbling and browned around the edges.

NOTE: Use a strongly flavoured cheese like mature Cheddar or Red Leicester or, even better, Gruyère or Emmental.
NOTE: The first stage of cooking, up to the end of step 2, can be done up to 24 hours in advance.

Medallions of Lamb with Roasted Garlic Sauce

Serves 6

675 g/1½ lb. fillet of lamb
salt and freshly ground black pepper
5 ml/1 tsp. crushed fresh rosemary, or 2.5 ml/½ tsp. dried
6 heads garlic, separated into cloves, skins left on
115 g/4 oz. butter
180–240 ml/6–8 fl. oz. light chicken stock
60 ml/4 tbsp. single cream

1. Heat the oven to 190°C/gas mark 5. Rub the lamb with salt, pepper and rosemary and leave on a plate to marinate. Place the cloves of garlic and the butter in a small ovenproof dish. Cover and bake for 50–60 minutes, basting occasionally, until the garlic is very soft.

2. Remove the garlic, (reserving the melted butter to use as a basis for a delicious pasta sauce!), and scrape out the pulp from the skins. In a food processor or liquidiser, work the garlic pulp and a little of the stock to a purée. Press it through a sieve to remove any fibres. Transfer to a small saucepan and whisk in more of the stock over a low heat until the mixture has a light pouring consistency. Whisk in the cream and season to taste with salt and pepper. Keep warm.

3. To cook the lamb, increase the oven temperature to 230°C/gas mark 8. Put the lamb in a roasting dish and cook for 15–18 minutes. Remove and let sit for 5 minutes, then cut into 1-cm/½-inch slices. Arrange in a circle on warmed individual plates, pour a ribbon of sauce around the outside of the lamb and place a small pile of sesame beans in the centre. (See next recipe.)

NOTE: Some supermarkets sell fillet of lamb ready-prepared; otherwise, ask the butcher to bone out some best end of lamb – the small chops used for crown roasts or 'guards of honour'. Do not cook the lamb longer than the time specified, which will leave the meat fairly pink and tender. The garlic sauce can be made up to 24 hours in advance and kept in the refrigerator, to be reheated at the last minute.

Sesame French Beans

Serves 6

675 g/1½ lb. French beans, washed and trimmed
300 ml/½ pint light chicken or vegetable stock
60 g/2 oz. butter
10 ml/2 tsp. sesame oil
15 ml/1 tbsp. toasted sesame seeds (see note)
10 ml/2 tsp. soy sauce
freshly ground black pepper

1. Cook the French beans in boiling stock until tender, drain and keep warm. Just before serving, toss the warm beans with the butter and sesame oil until well coated. Moisten the sesame seeds with the soy sauce and toss with the beans. Season to taste with pepper and serve immediately.

NOTE: Toast the sesame seeds by shaking from side to side in a hot dry frying pan for a few moments, or until they begin to turn a golden colour.

Easy Exotic Eats

Chilled Avocado and Coconut Soup
Prawns and Sole with Honey–chilli Sauce
Lychees in Green Ginger Wine

EXOTIC FOOD need not be difficult or time-consuming to prepare, and this meal, which requires very little skill, effort or time, is sure to delight and impress your guests. Although the recipes are certainly inspired by the various cuisines of Asia, they are far from 'authentic' and, whilst the flavours are decidedly Oriental, the meal is composed of ingredients that are easily available.

Chilled Avocado and Coconut Soup

Serves 6
3 ripe avocados
300 ml/ ½ pint coconut milk (see note)
450 ml/ ¾ pint light chicken stock (see note)
2 cloves garlic, peeled and crushed
2.5 ml/ ½ tsp. chilli powder
salt
45 ml/3 tbsp. lemon juice
30 ml/2 tbsp. chopped fresh coriander leaves or spring onions to garnish

1. Peel and stone the avocados and cut them into large chunks. Put all ingredients into a food processor or liquidiser and process until very smooth. Taste for seasoning and chill for at least 2 hours for flavours to blend. Serve with fresh coriander leaves or chopped spring onions as garnish.

110

NOTE: Coconut milk is usually available from Oriental grocers and some super-markets, but if you can't find it, soak 170 g/6 oz. desiccated coconut in 850 ml/1½ pint boiling water for 30 minutes. Pour it through a sieve, pressing hard to extract as much liquid as possible. This should produce about 600 ml/1 pint coconut milk.

NOTE: If you do not have any chicken stock and need to use a cube, look for the new variety which are made without additives. Not only are they better for your health, they taste decidedly better.

Prawns and Sole with Honey–chilli Sauce

Serves 6

1 onion, peeled and very finely chopped
1 clove garlic, peeled and crushed
30 ml/2 tbsp. vegetable oil
5 ml/1 tsp. ground coriander
2.5 ml/ ½ tsp. chilli powder
2.5 ml/ ½ tsp. salt
grated zest and juice of 1 lemon
180 ml/6 fl. oz. water
45 ml/3 tbsp. honey
12 cooked giant prawns, head and shells removed except for end of tail
450 g/1 lb. fillet of sole or plaice, skin removed, cut into 1-cm/ ½-inch strips
2 eggs, beaten
60 g/2 oz. white breadcrumbs
oil for frying

1. For the sauce, gently fry the onion and garlic in the oil until soft but not brown, 3–4 minutes. Add the coriander, chilli powder, salt, lemon zest and juice, the honey and the water and bring to a boil. Boil gently for 3–5 minutes, stirring frequently, until the sauce begins to thicken.

2. Dip the prawns and sole in the beaten egg and then in the breadcrumbs. In a frying pan, pour the oil to a depth of 1 cm/ ½ inch. Heat until hot, but not smoking and fry the sole and prawns until golden and crisp, 1–2 minutes on each side. Drain on kitchen paper, arrange on individual plates and spoon a little sauce over.

NOTE: If you can buy uncooked prawns, so much the better. An excellent and cheaper substitute for prawns is monk-fish, cut into 2.5-cm/1-inch cubes.

Lychees in Green Ginger Wine

Serves 6

2 × 570 g/1 lb. 4 oz. tins lychees, drained
240 ml/8 fl. oz. green ginger wine

1. Drain the lychees. Put them in a bowl with the wine and marinate for 2 hours. Serve chilled.

Cruditiés and Quail Eggs with Avocado Dip and Mustard Soured Cream Dip (*see page 114*). A large meat platter is ideal for arranging this colourful dish, but, as it is completely covered by food, it does not have to be anything special – a tray will do just as well, or even a baking sheet covered with kitchen foil.

Speedy Stand-up Supper

**Crudités and Quail Eggs with Avocado
Dip and Mustard Soured Cream Dip
Hot Bacon-wrapped Fruit and Marinated Sausage Bites
Grape and Gruyère Sticks
'Many Treasure' Prawn Salad
Mixed Bean Salad
Tomatoes in Virgin Olive Oil
Pitta Bread
Raspberry Mousse**

THERE ARE lots of occasions when a sizeable group of people want to get together to celebrate with a shared meal, but when time and place allow for only the minimum planning and preparation – whether it is the end of term party for your upholstery evening class or a last-minute office binge to celebrate a colleague's engagement or promotion.

A menu with lots of different, though simple, dishes will give sufficient variety of foods to make a lavish 'spread'. A carefully planned and balanced menu is essential, and careful delegation will ensure that no one person ends up with too much to do or worry about.

The following menu is designed for an occasion when it won't necessarily be possible for the guests to sit down with a knife and fork in front of them but when just 'finger food' to accompany the drinks is not enough. The first half of the meal, however, is intended to be 'picked at' while the guests all arrive or assemble and mill around chatting over their first drinks. A couple of hot 'nibbles' herald the arrival of the more substantial part of the menu in which three salads, whilst easy to eat with just a fork, provide a proper meal on a plate.

The pudding, although easy to make, is the only part of the meal which requires much advance preparation. If you want to make things even simpler, you can instead serve bought cakes or gâteaux or just fresh fruit.

Quantities for this kind of a meal are difficult to give, as you will perhaps want to vary the menu according to the situation, perhaps substituting the hot dishes for something else if you do not have cooking facilities available on the occasion. Where I have given precise recipes, I have suggested quantities to feed 12 people, but these are simple to adapt for more or less people.

Crudités and Quail Eggs with Avocado Dip and Mustard Soured Cream Dip

Arrange a selection of sticks of raw vegetables on serving platters with bowls of hard-boiled quails eggs and dips in the middle or in separate bowls near by.

I use carrots, celery, red, green and yellow pepper, radishes and leaves of chicory. Bread sticks, crisps, small savoury biscuits and corn chips are also good to dip.

Quail eggs are now becoming much more readily available and can be found in many big supermarkets. To hard-boil, place in a suitable pan in cold water, bring to the boil and simmer for 3 minutes. Drain and cool in cold water. They are a little fiddly to shell, but I remove the shells from most of them, leaving a few with the shells on as they are so pretty. Allow 3–4 per person.

Serve with Avocado Dip (see below) and/or Mustard Soured Cream Dip.

For the Mustard Soured Cream Dip, simply mix dry English mustard to taste with soured cream and season well with salt and freshly ground black pepper.

Avocado Dip

3 large, very ripe, but not bruised, avocados, peeled and stoned

juice of 2 lemons

3 cloves garlic, peeled and crushed

salt and freshly ground black pepper

bottled mild chilli sauce (chilli and ginger is good)

Mash the avocados with the lemon and garlic in a bowl and add salt and pepper and chilli sauce to taste. If you have a food processor, simply add all the ingredients and blend until smooth.

Serve with crisps, corn chips or sticks of raw vegetables (as above) – or, if you are feeling extravagant, it is delicious with giant prawns.

Hot Bacon-wrapped Fruit and Marinated Sausage Bites

Cut thin rashers of streaky bacon in half across and wrap around small cubes of firm fruit securing with wooden cocktail sticks. Fresh or tinned fruit can be used, but not soft fruit like strawberries or raspberries. I use 'mixed tropical fruit' in light syrup. This contains neat cubes of pineapple, papaya and watermelon. Tinned pineapple in natural juice would also be good and very convenient. Grill for about 2–3 minutes each side or until crisp and browned.

For the Sausage Bites, simply prick sausages of your choice on both sides with the prongs of a fork and lay them in a shallow dish. Pour over a bought bottled marinade and leave for about an hour, turning occasionally before grilling. There are lots of excellent ready-prepared marinade mixes now avaiable in bottles. I like chilli and garlic.

When the sausages are cooked, simply cut each one across into 4 pieces and serve with wooden cocktail sticks to pick them up with. Grill for about 2–3 minutes each side or until crisp and browned.

Grape and Gruyère Sticks

Cut 2-cm/1inch cubes of Gruyère cheese (Emmental is just as nice, or even Cheddar or Edam) and spear on to wooden cocktail sticks, each accompanied by one black or green seedless grape. This is a perfect job for children.

'Many Treasure' Prawn Salad

Makes 12 small or 8 large servings

450 g/1 lb. shelled prawns, thawed if frozen
1 × 225 g/8 oz. tin Chinese water chestnuts, drained and halved
1 × 575 g/1¼ lb. tin Chinese lychees, drained and halved (save juice for a drink)
½ cucumber, wiped and cut into 1-cm/½-inch cubes
1 bunch spring onions, trimmed and chopped (green part included)
60 ml/4 tbsp. good quality mayonnaise
grated rind of ½ lemon
1 clove garlic, peeled and crushed
1-cm/½-inch cube fresh ginger, very finely chopped or crushed through a garlic press.
2.5–5 ml/½–1 tsp. chilli powder (according to taste)
salt and freshly ground black pepper
3 bulbs stem ginger in syrup, drained and finely chopped (optional)

1. Combine first 5 ingredients in a bowl.
2. Flavour the mayonnaise with the remaining ingredients except stem ginger and stir well into the prawn mixture. Garnish with stem ginger (if used).

Serve with tinned Mixed Bean Salad (there are many different brands available – I use a supermarket's own brand and find it excellent; allow 1 large tin for 4–6 portions depending on appetites) and sliced tomatoes (allow 1 medium-large tomato per person, dressed with virgin olive oil, a little lemon juice, salt and freshly ground black pepper and any chopped fresh herb you fancy). Hot pitta bread goes very well with this but any other good bread would be fine.

115

Raspberry Mousse

Makes 8 large or 12 small servings

675 g/1½ lb. raspberries, thawed if frozen
60 ml/4 tbsp. sugar, or more to taste
2 sachets powdered gelatine
120 ml/4 fl. oz. water
900 ml/1½ pints whipping or double cream
mint leaves (optional)

1. Purée the fruit with the sugar in a food processor or liquidiser and transfer to a bowl. If you mind the seeds, sieve the purée. I don't bother.
2. Dissolve the gelatine in the water according to the instructions on the packet, and add to the purée.
3. Whip 600 ml/1 pint of the cream until light and thick, but not too stiff, and fold into the purée. Pour into a suitable serving bowl or individual dishes or glasses. Chill until set (at least 4 hours and up to 24).
4. Whip the remaining cream till stiff and use to decorate the top of the mousse. Pipe it if you want, but I just blob it around the edge with a spoon. Garnish with the mint leaves (if used).

Barbecue on a Budget

Grilled Chicken Wings in Ginger and Garlic Marinade
Lamburgers, with Fresh Herbed Melon Relish
Mixed Meat and Vegetable Kebabs
Green Salad with Garlic and Grapefruit Dressing
Pasta and Spring Onion Salad with
Mustard–lemon Mayonnaise

I ENJOYED my first taste of really good barbecued food in sunny Australia, where the locals have perfected this outdoor cooking method down to a fine art.

Down Under, of course, they are blessed with frequent sunshine and wonderful raw ingredients, which make *al fresco* cooking and eating a natural and wonderfully informal way to entertain.

On this side of the world, however, we sometimes are blessed with sunny days, but the price of the sort of cuts of meat the Aussies like to throw on the 'barbie' make for a very expensive occasion if you are feeding more than just a few.

An inexpensive barbecued meal is not impossible, and this menu provides a really hearty spread, with lots of variety, for an amazingly small cost.

Shopping around for inexpensive meat, rather than just buying it in the first supermarket you come to, can provide enormous savings, particularly if you are feeding a crowd, as many butchers offer greatly reduced prices for bulk buys, particularly with things like chicken wings. If your butcher doesn't normally sell minced lamb, ask him to mince it for you and if you are buying quite a lot (you can freeze some burgers once you have made them) he might give you a 'special' price if you ask nicely.

Lamburgers and
Mixed Meat and
Vegetable Kebabs
(*see over*).

119

Grilled Chicken Wings in Ginger and Garlic Marinade

Serves 12

5 ml/1 tsp. ground ginger
10 ml/2 tsp. soy sauce
2 cloves garlic, peeled and crushed
10 ml 2 tsp. sugar
salt and freshly ground black pepper
30 ml/2 tbsp. vinegar (wine or cider vinegar is best, but malt is fine)
30 ml/2 tbsp. vegetable oil
12 chicken wings, thawed if frozen

1. Put the ginger, soy sauce, garlic and sugar, with salt and pepper to taste, in a bowl. Pour on the vinegar, and whisk until dissolved. Whisk in the oil and add the chicken wings, mixing well and turning until well coated with the marinade.
2. Cover with a plate, or cling film and leave to marinate from 1–24 hours, stirring and turning as often as possible. If you can only leave the meat for up to 2 hours, do this at room temperature; if longer, keep the bowl in the fridge.
3. Grill on a hot barbecue (or grill in inclement weather) for about 15–20 minutes, or until cooked through.

Lamburgers

Serves 12

1 kg/2 lb. minced lamb
4 cloves garlic, peeled and crushed
60 ml/4 tbsp. finely chopped parsley
10 ml/2 tsp. finely chopped or crumbled dried rosemary (add 50 per cent more if using fresh)
grated rind of 1 lemon
salt and freshly ground black pepper
12 soft burger buns (or similar) split around the equator

1. Mix all the ingredients very thoroughly by hand in a large bowl. If you wish to test the seasonings, break off a piece and fry in a pan until cooked, then taste.
2. Divide the mixture into 12 equal portions and shape with wetted hands, first into balls, then flat into a burger shape. A good way to get the burgers perfectly round and all the same size is to press them into a wetted round pastry-cutter, on a wetted work surface. Simply lift off the pastry-cutter and you will be left with a perfect, professional-looking burger.
3. At this stage the burgers are quite fragile and are much easier to handle if chilled. They can be made up to 24 hours in advance and left in the fridge until the last minute. Lift them carefully on to a baking sheet with a fish slice and chill for at least 2 hours. If you are making a large quantity, you can stack the burgers in piles, with a square of baking parchment or greaseproof paper between each one to prevent them sticking together.
4. To cook, place the burgers carefully on the hot barbecue and cook for about 15 minutes, turning once. Alternatively, fry or cook under an ordinary grill.
5. Serve each one sandwiched in a split roll. These can be toasted if you prefer.

Offer the following relish, or alternatively, bottled barbecue sauce, chilli sauce, mint jelly or whatever else you fancy.

Fresh Herbed Melon Relish

Yields approximately 25 servings

1 small melon
1 large or 2 small onions, peeled
5 ml/1 tsp. ginger (or more to taste)
salt and freshly ground black pepper
4 cloves garlic, peeled and crushed
juice of ½ lemon
30 ml/2 tbsp. finely chopped parsley
10 ml/2 tsp. finely chopped fresh mint (if available)

1. Cut melon in half and remove the seeds. Scoop out all the flesh with a spoon and finely chop. Place in a bowl.
2. Very finely chop the onion and add to the melon. Sprinkle with the ginger and season well with salt and pepper.
3. Mix in the garlic, lemon juice, parsley and mint (if used).

NOTE: This relish is fine if made at the last minute, but can be made up to 6 hours in advance. In which case, if you find that it has become too 'wet' drain in a colander for a few minutes before putting in a serving bowl.

If you fancy something more fiery, add chopped fresh green chilli to taste.

Mixed Meat and Vegetable Kebabs

Serves 12

Juice of 1 lemon
30 ml/2 tbsp. vegetable oil
5 ml/1 tsp. dried sage, or 10 ml/2 tsp. chopped fresh
salt and freshly ground black pepper
6 thin, rindless rashers of streaky bacon (I prefer smoked)
2 firm bananas
235 g/8 oz. boneless turkey (I used turkey escalopes from a supermarket)
12 cocktail sausages
½ red pepper and ½ green pepper (or whatever colours are available)
1 small onion, peeled and chopped

1. Mix together in a bowl the first 4 ingredients to make a marinade.
2. Stretch the bacon rashers a little with the back of a knife, cut them in half crossways and reserve. You will have 12 longish bits.
3. Peel the bananas and cut each crossways into 6 even chunks. Put immediately into the bowl with the marinade and toss thoroughly but gently to coat.
4. Cut the turkey into 12 even bits and add to the marinade. Toss to coat. Leave at room temperature for about 30 minutes, but no longer than an hour.
5. Cut the peppers into 24 pieces, 12 of each colour, discarding any seeds, and reserve.
6. Cut the onion into 12 even chunks.
7. Remove the banana pieces from the marinade and wrap each one in a piece of bacon. The loose ends will be secured by the skewer or stick.
8. Remove the turkey pieces from the marinade and put on a plate.

9. Assemble the kebabs by threading the ingredients on to 12 metal skewers or wooden or bamboo ones, which have been first soaked in water for at least an hour, to prevent them from burning when placed over the hot charcoal. Arrange them to look attractive, but each should have 1 piece of turkey, 1 sausage and 1 bacon/banana roll, interspersed with 2 pieces of pepper and a piece of onion.

10. To cook, grill for about 15 minutes over hot charcoal, turning once, and basting halfway through the cooking time with any remaining marinade. Alternatively, cook under an ordinary grill.

Green Salad with Garlic and Grapefruit Dressing

Serves 12

1 large Cos or other firm lettuce, or equivalent quantity of mixed salad leaves weighing approximately 450 g/1 lb.

Dressing

30 ml/2 tbsp. freshly squeezed grapefruit juice

90 ml/6 tbsp. corn oil

5 ml/1 tsp. sugar

2 cloves garlic, peeled and crushed

salt and freshly ground black pepper

1. Wash, drain and shred the lettuce leaves. This can be done up to 2 hours in advance if leaves are kept in a closed plastic bag in a cool place.

2. Shake the dressing ingredients together in a screw-topped jar or other convenient container until well amalgamated. This can be prepared up to 24 hours in advance and kept in the fridge.

3. At the last minute, put the leaves in a suitable bowl and pour over the dressing. Toss lightly but thoroughly.

NOTE: If you are not too keen on garlic, you can substitute 5 ml/1 tsp. English mustard powder, 5 ml/1 tsp. ready-made horseradish sauce (or more to taste), or some snipped chives or other fresh herbs.

Pasta and Spring Onion Salad with Mustard–lemon Mayonnaise

Yields 40 × 15 ml/1 tbsp. servings

500 g/1 lb. dried pasta corkscrews (or whatever shape you fancy – mixed colours look very party-ish)
1 bunch spring onions, trimmed and finely chopped
2 eggs
5 ml/1 tsp. English mustard powder
5 ml/1 tsp. salt (or more according to taste)
360 ml/12fl. oz. vegetables oil (I use corn oil)
juice of 1 small lemon
60 ml/4 tbsp. finely chopped parsley, plus extra for garnish

1. Cook the pasta according to the instructions on the packet. Drain and plunge into cold water, leave for a few minutes to cool and drain again. Dry on clean tea towels. Reserve while you make the mayonnaise.

2. Put the whole eggs in the bowl of a food processor or liquidiser with the mustard, salt and pepper to taste; process for 10 seconds. With the motor running, add the oil in a thin steady stream. When all the oil is added, you should have a thick, unctuous mayonnaise. If it is too thin, add more oil until the desired thickness is achieved. It should be fairly thick, as the lemon juice will dilute it.

3. Add the lemon juice and parsley and blend for a few more seconds.

4. Check the seasoning. It should be very tasty.

5. Mix the cold pasta with the mayonnaise and chopped spring onions and put into a serving bowl. Sprinkle with the extra parsley. Cover with cling film if you are not ready to use it.

NOTE: This salad can be made up to 24 hours in advance.

NOTE: These quantities are for a whole 500 g/1 lb packet of pasta. You can of course make less – just adjust the quantities accordingly.

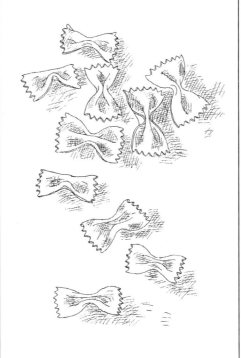

Children's DIY Pizza Party

DIY Pizzas
Carrot Sticks and Corn Chips
with Tomato–mayonnaise Dip
Stuffed Cherry Tomatoes
See-through Sandwiches
Ice Cream
Fizzy 'Spider' Jelly
'Real' Orange Jelly Wedges
Chocolate Strawberries
Frozen Grapes

ALL CHILDREN love parties and most children love party food. Younger ones are quite happy with simple traditional party tea-time fare and will be enchanted by biscuits with funny faces or their names iced on to them and be amused by childish games. Older children, however, from seven years onwards, are now surprisingly sophisticated and it will take a much more imaginative birthday production to impress them.

'Grown-up' savoury foods like hot dogs, burgers or 'chicken bites' are likely to go down much better than 'rabbit' jellies and fairy cakes with this age group, although any original or amusing food presentation will be greatly appreciated.

For all children's parties the food is but a small part of the proceedings if the party is to be a memorable one and the games, activities, entertainments and other diversions are more likely to be remembered than the eats. Although such treats as conjurors, video films or outings will always be highly successful, old-fashioned games like musical chairs, Statues and Pass the Parcel never fail to please, just as jelly and ice cream will never really go out of favour.

The DIY pizza in the menu suggested here gives children the kind of food they like but it also becomes more than just a meal. The involvement with the cooking also keeps the guests amused in an original way at the beginning of the party, and should help to break the ice for shyer children.

This kind of party is ideal for a small group of 6–8 youngsters, in your own

DIY Pizzas (*see over*).

125

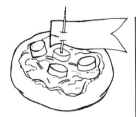

home, but if you have access to, or can hire, a hall or other venue with suitable cooking facilities attached, up to 30 children can be catered for quite easily with a little careful organisation and a few adult helpers.

If you find the right venue, but it doesn't have sufficient available oven space to cook so many pizzas, baked potatoes with a selection of different toppings to choose from make a good alternative, particularly if you can borrow 2 or 3 microwaves from friends for the occasion.

The menu given here is merely offered as a guideline. No doubt your offspring will have their own very definite opinions about which other culinary 'musts' will also be essential on the birthday tea table.

Lastly, don't get into a flap if you aren't very good at baking – get a friend who is to help with the cake or buy one ready-made. The candle ceremony is much more important than the cake itself!

DIY Pizzas

Serves 6

1 × 280 g/10 oz. packet 'white bread and pizza base mix' (available from most large supermarkets)
15 ml/1 tbsp. vegetable oil
1 small onion, peeled and chopped
395 g/14 oz. tin tomatoes, drained and chopped
pinch of dried mixed herbs
salt and freshly ground black pepper
60 g/2 oz. chopped ham, or two cooked sausages cut across into 1-cm/½-inch slices (or both)
60 g/2 oz. button mushrooms, sliced
½ small red, yellow or green pepper, seeded and chopped (a mixture looks good if you are feeding large numbers)
small 200 g/7 oz tin sweetcorn, drained
115 g/4 oz. cheddar cheese, grated
30 ml/2 tbsp. chopped parsley

1. Heat the oil in a medium sized saucepan and cook the onion over a moderate heat until soft and transparent, stirring occasionally. Add the drained tomatoes, herbs and pepper and salt to taste and bring to the boil. Reduce the heat to low and simmer, uncovered for 10 minutes, stirring occasionally. Transfer to a bowl, cover with cling film and leave to cool.

2. Make dough according to the instructions on the packet. It is even quicker if you have a food processor, and just needs to be processed for 1 minute with the plastic blade.

3. Divide dough into 6 equal portions and roll each out into a 14-cm/5½-inch circle. Place on a greased baking tray, cover loosely with cling film and leave to rise in a warm place for about 15 minutes. (This can be done earlier in the day as the dough can be kept in the fridge for up to 4 hours.)

4. Place all the topping ingredients in separate bowls or on plates and arrange in a line for the children to add whatever combination they like to their pizza. (Advise them to start with the tomato sauce as this stops the other ingredients from falling straight off – alternatively the bases could be spread with the tomato sauce in advance.)

5. Bake in a preheated oven 220°C/ gas mark 7 for about 15 minutes or until cooked.

NOTE: This is just a suggestion for toppings: you can use additional items such as shrimps, chopped pineapple, slices of salami, etc. Best to have more than enough, because any left-overs can be used up for stir-fries, sandwiches or omelette fillings.

Some means of identification is a very good idea for when the pizzas come out of the oven, such as little greaseproof paper flags speared on to wooden cocktail sticks, on which the children can write their names in non-toxic crayons, and then spike into their own 'creations'.

Carrot Sticks and Corn Chips with Tomato–mayonnaise Dip

carrots, washed and peeled (if you wish)

corn chips

mayonnaise

tomato ketchup

1. Cut carrots into conveniently sized 'sticks' and arrange around a plate with the corn chips.

2. Mix the mayonnaise with a little ketchup to colour and flavour it and fill a suitable bowl. Place this in the middle of the serving plate.

Stuffed Cherry Tomatoes

Makes 12 tomatoes

12 cherry tomatoes (choose larger ones)

2 hard-boiled eggs, shelled and mashed or finely chopped

15 ml/1 tbsp. mayonnaise

1. Cut a small 'cap' off the rounded side (the 'navel' side will become the base) of the tomatoes and reserve. Carefully remove the flesh and seeds with a small sharp knife and then a small sharp teaspoon and discard.

2. Mix the egg with the mayonnaise and spoon into the tomatoes. Perch 'caps' back on top at an angle to show filling and arrange on a plate.

Fizzy 'Spider' Jelly (*see over*). Clear plastic glasses or cups are perfect for these so that the children can see what 'horrors' are suspended in their jelly!

See-through Sandwiches

white bread

sandwich filling of your choice

1. Cut shapes out of the centre of half the slices of bread with suitable pastry cutters (animals, hearts, aeroplanes, etc.) discarding cut-outs (give discarded bits to the birds). Spread filling on the other slices and then place 'see-through' slices on top. Cut off crusts.

NOTE: The filling must not be too pale or the cut-outs won't show up enough. I use tinned tuna fish, moistened with mayonnaise and coloured with tomato ketchup (a wonderful standby for children's food). Jam, of course, is simple and would work perfectly.

Fizzy 'Spider' Jelly

fizzy lemonade

gelatine

gruesome jelly sweets, e.g., spiders, worms, sharks, etc.

1. Put lemonade in the freezer to get as cold as possible without actually freezing.
2. Dissolve gelatine in a little water according to the instructions on the packet. Add the really cold lemonade using the proportions 3 sachets of gelatine to 2 pints of liquid.
3. Fill suitable glasses half full and place immediately in fridge until nearly set.
4. Just before jellies set, add gruesome jelly spider/worm/shark to each glass and replace in fridge until set.
5. Repeat steps 1 and 2 and then fill glasses to top. Replace in fridge till set.

NOTE: Because the lemonade is so cold, and the proportion of gelatine to liquid high, the jellies should set almost immediately, trapping the bubbles and leaving the jelly fizzy. Quite an odd taste sensation if you have never experienced it!

'Real' Orange Jelly Wedges

Serves 8

2 large oranges

orange juice (the pure unsweetened kind in cartons is best

1 sachet gelatine

20 ml/1 heaped tbsp. sugar (or more to taste)

1. Cut oranges in half and scoop out the flesh. Squeeze the juice from the flesh and strain into a measuring jug (or purée in liquidiser or food processor and strain through sieve). Discard pulp in sieve. Reserve orange 'shells'.
2. Make up to 1 pint/600 ml with orange juice.
3. Make jelly with juice, sugar and gelatine according to the instructions on the packet, and fill the orange 'shells'. Chill until set.
4. Cut jelly orange 'shells' into two equal wedges, and arrange in a circle on a plate.

Chocolate Strawberries

strawberries (green leafy stalk left on)

milk chocolate (140 g/5 oz. chocolate for every 395 g/1 lb. strawberries)

1. Melt chocolate in a bowl over a pan of gently simmering water. Be careful not to let any water get into chocolate.
2. Holding strawberries by the green part, dip them one by one in the melted chocolate, but only halfway. Arrange on a small tray or board, covered with greaseproof paper or kitchen parchment and chill until set.

NOTE: You can also use white chocolate. These are best made not longer than 3–4 hours beforehand.

Frozen Grapes

Freeze seedless grapes for not less than 6 hours. Remove from freezer 5 minutes before serving.

131

Index